spiritualintimacy

drawing closer to God

Glen Martin and Dian Ginter

LifeWay Christian Resources
Nashville, Tennessee

Produced by: National Student Ministry Department
LifeWay Christian Resources • 127 Ninth Avenue North • Nashville, Tennessee 37234 • Customer Service: (800) 458-BSSB

Editor: Art Herron
Production Specialist: Leanne B. Adams
Graphic Designer: Bob Redden

© Copyright 1999 by LifeWay. All rights reserved. Printed in the United States of America.

CrossSeekers™, Be More™, CrossSeekers logo, CrossSeekers person figure, and the six Covenant icons are all trademarks of LifeWay Christian Resources. All rights reserved.

Dewey Decimal Classification: 248.834
Subject Heading: Spiritual Life/Youth—Religious Life

This study is based on *Drawing Closer* by Glen Martin and Dian Ginter.
Published by Broadman and Holman Publishers, 127 Ninth Avenue North, Nashville, Tennessee 37234. © Copyright 1995 by Broadman and Holman Publishers.

Scripture quotations are from the Holy Bible, *New International Version,* copyright © 1973, 1978, 1984 by International Bible Society. Used by permission.

ISBN 0-7673-9427-5

contents

about the writers 4

the crossseekers covenant 5

introduction 6

session one
God is sovereign 10

session two
God came as sacrificial Savior 24

session three
God cares as a loving father 36

session four
God stays with you as a faithful companion . . . 50

session five
God demonstrates friendship 64

session six
God becomes your intimate friend 76

leader's guide 90

crossseekers resources 94

spiritualintimacy
drawing closer to God

about the writers

Dr. Glen S. Martin is senior pastor of Community Baptist Church in Manhattan Beach, California, an innovative leader in establishing new models of ministry in the Southern California area. Glen is currently a speaker and seminar leader with Promise Keepers, Man in the Mirror, Ministry Track Seminars, and The Center for Leadership Development in Canada, speaking on the subjects of leadership, change, small groups, evangelism, and assimilation. He is also an adjunct professor at Talbot School of Theololy, Biola University. Dr. Martin has authored numerous books and articles, including his latest two books, ***Creating Community*** and ***Your Pastor's Heart,*** with Moody Press. ***God's Top Ten List*** is scheduled to be released by Moody Press in 1999. Glen and his wife Nancy live in Hermosa Beach and have three children: Kerry, Scott, and David.

***Martin and Ginter previously co-authored* Power House: A Step-by-Step Guide to Building a Church that Prays.**

Dian Ginter went home to be with the Lord on October 1, 1998. Her passion was for prayer and for helping others deepen their walk with Jesus. This book is a wonderful tribute to Dian and our work that all may be *Drawing Closer* each day to our Lord and Savior, Jesus Christ.

Galatians 6:9

—Dr. Glen Martin

The CrossSeekers™ Covenant

"You will seek me and find me when you seek me with all your heart." Jeremiah 29:13

As a seeker of the cross of Christ, I am called to break away from trite, nonchalant, laissez-faire Christian living. I accept the challenge to divine daring, to consecrated recklessness for Christ, to devout adventure in the face of ridiculing contemporaries. Created in the image of God and committed to excellence as a disciple of Jesus Christ,

INTEGRITY

I will be a person of integrity
"Do your best to present yourself to God as one approved, a workman who does not need to be ashamed and who correctly handles the word of truth." 2 Timothy 2:15

My attitudes and actions reveal my commitment to live the kind of life Christ modeled for me—to speak the truth in love, to stand firm in my convictions, to be honest and trustworthy.

SPIRITUAL GROWTH

I will pursue consistent spiritual growth
"So then, just as you received Christ Jesus as Lord, continue to live in him, rooted and built up in him, strengthened in the faith as you were taught, and overflowing with thankfulness." Colossians 2:6-7

The Christian life is a continuing journey, and I am committed to a consistent, personal relationship with Jesus Christ, to faithful study of His Word, and to regular corporate spiritual growth through the ministry of the New Testament church.

WITNESS

I will speak and live a relevant, authentic, and consistent witness
"Always be prepared to give an answer to everyone who asks you to give the reason for the hope that you have." 1 Peter 3:15

I will tell others the story of how Jesus changed my life, and I will seek to live a radically changed life each day. I will share the good news of Jesus Christ with courage and boldness.

SERVICE

I will seek opportunities to serve in Christ's name
"The Spirit of the Lord is on me, because he has anointed me to preach good news to the poor. He has sent me to proclaim freedom for the prisoners and recovery of sight for the blind, to release the oppressed, to proclaim the year of the Lord's favor." Luke 4:18-19

I believe that God desires to draw all people into a loving, redeeming relationship with Him. As His disciple, I will give myself to be His hands to reach others in ministry and missions.

PURITY

I will honor my body as the temple of God, dedicated to a lifestyle of purity
"Do you not know that your body is a temple of the Holy Spirit, who is in you, whom you have received from God? You are not your own; you were bought at a price. Therefore honor God with your body." 1 Corinthians 6:19-20

Following the example of Christ, I will keep my body healthy and strong, avoiding temptations and destructive personal vices. I will honor the gift of life by keeping myself sexually pure and free from addictive drugs.

CHRISTLIKE RELATIONSHIPS

I will be godly in all things, Christlike in all relationships
"Therefore, as God's chosen people, holy and dearly loved, clothe yourselves with compassion, kindness, humility, gentleness and patience. Bear with each other and forgive whatever grievances you may have against one another. Forgive as the Lord forgave you. And over all these virtues put on love, which binds them all together in perfect unity." Colossians 3:12-14

In every relationship and in every situation, I will seek to live as Christ would. I will work to heal brokenness, to value each person as a child of God, to avoid petty quarrels and harsh words, to let go of bitterness and resentment that hinder genuine Christian love.

Copyright © 1998 LifeWay Publications. CrossSeekers is a ministry of National Student Ministry. For more information, visit our Web site: **www.crossseekers.org**.

INTRODUCTION

Why Should I Draw Closer to God?

Have you ever seen a Christian friend who had such a wonderful relationship with the Lord that you were almost envious? Maybe you thought to yourself, *"Oh, how I wish I knew God in that way. I could never hear from God like my friend does. I can never be as close to God as this person. I will never be good enough for God to let me be that close to Him."* Such puzzling thoughts are not uncommon among believers. We doubt ourselves and we doubt our worth before God.

But are the conclusions right? Not at all. Why? God created us with the need for relationship. We need God and we need other people. We need to feel appreciated, important, and significant to God and to others. So your longing to draw near to God is as right as rain. Amazingly, He wants to draw close to you as well. For many people, this concept is like a giant, complicated God-puzzle. We have lots of pieces, but no picture of how the puzzle should be put together. Throughout the centuries, people have tried putting their pieces together. Most often they come up with distorted, unsatisfying pictures that never fill the needs in their lives.

Let God help you put the pieces together.

Those who put the pieces together correctly soon notice that it takes the shape of a road. This is the road of life. God is with you on the road, desiring to accompany you, to show you the best path, and to point out the obstacles. The picture is one that, when completed, will be your life. God is involved in every part, every aspect. Each day has puzzle pieces to be put in, and perhaps misplaced pieces to correct. As you take the puzzle pieces of your life, each day will bring a fuller understanding of who God is and who we are. You understand more of who God is as you see Him work in your life, as you learn more about Him from His Word—the Bible—and as you obey Him in a deeper, more trusting way. These are important pieces of God helping you put your puzzle together.

Many people realize that having an intimate friendship with God is possible. They even know the words to say. However, few people know how to actually grow this relationship with God. In fact, most people don't know their own level of relationship with God. They don't know how to get from where they are to the closeness they want. The purpose of this study is to help you, as CrossSeekers, understand the levels of knowing God, to identify where you are in this process, and to give effective suggestions on how to get from where you are to where you want to be. In essence, the purpose of this study is to learn how to solve the God-puzzle.

As you work through this study, hopefully you will have the following experiences:
- Glimpse what you have been missing.
- Catch a vision of the great relationship you can have with God.
- Find motivation to take the steps from where you are to deeper closeness with God.
- Enjoy the pure pleasure in getting to know our Awesome, Personal God.
- Understand how to take steps to intimacy with God, and start to do just that.
- No longer feel confused about the God-puzzle, but be confident that your picture of God will grow more accurate with each day.

You've Got the Yearning

God has placed a desire for Himself within every human heart. Romans 1 in the Bible explains two ways to know God: we know about God's existence from external evidences such as nature, and also from internal encounters with God. Each person chooses how to respond to such knowledge. Those who choose to pursue God, find Him. The rewards are great. Those who ignore Him create all kinds of personal turmoil for themselves.

Why do you want to pursue God rather than push Him away? Write your answers in the space provided here.

Start by:
- Discovering that He exists;
- Choosing to accept salvation;
- Choosing actions and attitudes that bring you closer to Him each day;
- Seeing how He wants to put your life together.

God Invites You to Come Close

God has provided everything necessary for the most intimate relationship with Him. God wants you to get to know Him better. So the last part of growing that relationship is you. The better you know Him, the more you can trust Him. As you see His great capabilities and respond to His power working in and through your life, He becomes more precious to you. Then as you draw closer, you want to trust and obey Him more. You develop a heart for God. This heart attitude plays a pivotal role in determining how close you will draw to God and at what rate. God even helps you grow this heart attitude. Come join the adventure!

Intimacy with God is an ongoing process. The key is learning more about who God really is. As you learn who God really is, you see what He does. You learn how much He loves you and how His heart responds to you. You discover why obeying Him brings absolute freedom.

As you learn these things and they sink deeply into you heart and soul, your trust in God grows. You want to spend more time with God, not because you ought to, but because your heart is awakening. You begin to long for time to spend with your Creator. And amazingly, you discover that you can spend all 24 hours of every day doing just that!

God Cares About You Continually

In Jeremiah 29:11-14*a* God says, " *'For I know the plans I have for you,' declares the Lord, 'plans to prosper you and not to harm you, plans to give you hope and a future. Then you will call upon me and come and pray to me, and I will listen to you. You will seek me and find me when you seek* *me with all your heart. I will be found by you,' declares the Lord."*

Circle five words that mean the most to you in the previous passage. Then jot them here:
_____ _____ _____ _____ _____

Lloyd Ogilvie describes the beauty of this Jeremiah passage:

> "Imagine someone you love and admire and whose thoughts and opinions you cherish, saying to you, 'You are constantly on my mind. And when I think of you they are wonderful thoughts of peace and future happiness for you. I'm pulling for the very best for you. What a joy it is to be your cheerleader!' It would not be difficult to find time for conversation with a person like that. Multiply the best of human care and concern for us a billion times and you've only begun to fathom God's love for us as He calls us into conversation."

Each time you let God speak to you, you let Him love you!

As you begin this study, talk to God with these words from Psalm 63:1-8:

O God, you are my God, earnestly I seek you; my soul thirsts for you, my body longs for you, in a dry and weary land where there is no water. I have seen you in the sanctuary and beheld your power and your glory. Because your love is better than life, my lips will glorify you. I will praise you as long as I live, and in your name I will lift up my hands. My soul will be satisfied as with the richest of foods; with singing lips my mouth will praise you. On my bed I remember you; I think of you through the watches of the night. Because you are my help, I sing in the shadow of your wings. My soul clings to you; your right hand upholds me.

Delight Awaits You

Are you a little overwhelmed thinking about the task before you? Don't be. Catch the vision for what God wants in your relationship with Him as a Christian and as a CrossSeeker. The journey is worth taking. Like any journey there are both fears and thrills. As you take the necessary steps toward a deeper, more intimate relationship with God, you will be amazed. Each step you take will bring its own satisfaction, and the rewards will be overwhelming and awesome. Let yourself draw closer to God.

This is not suggesting that reaching any level of intimacy with God brings perfection or that you will eventually be without problems. Quite the contrary is true. There is always selfishness and temptation to contend with, always the weaknesses inherent in our humanity. But our weaknesses do not have to dominate us. As CrossSeekers, you and God can control them.

It is also true that God will shine His light on some of those dark corners of your life that you have hidden. Even though this will bring its own struggles, you will find deeper joy as you allow Him to remove these hindrances and distractions in your life.

A Sunday School teacher once asked her students to talk about how they felt about their church. The students responded in the usual ways. Some of them said silly things to get the rest of the class to laugh. Other students tried to be more serious with their answers. One of the new girls in the class said that going to church was "like walking into the heart of God."

What a thought! To be in the very heart of God! Yet this is what He offers you each time you approach Him with the proper attitude and desire to know Him better. You will find the results of drawing closer to God are life-changing. Your heart will seek the things of God. Your joy in daily life and in relationships with people will deepen. How much will your life change as you begin to seek the things of God through this CrossSeekers study? Come find out.

Encourage Your Group: Actions for Group Study

At the end of each chapter are specific items to discuss with your group. These help you help each other go deeper in your relationships with God. In addition to these suggestions, feel free to discuss the questions throughout each chapter. Each session also includes a group-leading tip. Find even more tips in the Leader's Guide at the back of this book.

Between You and God

At the end of each chapter are also activities for personal reflection. These include Scripture to read, ways to reflect on what you discovered in that session, and ideas for preparing for the next week's study. These activities supplement the questions throughout each chapter. In this section you will complete a personal evaluation of where you are on that level of intimacy with God.

You may want to complete all the personal evaluations at the beginning of this study and then again at the end to see your progress as you grow in your relationship with God.

Listen to the lyrics to "Trust" from the album *smalltown poets* by smalltown poets

(Ardent Music, 1997).

- What hunger does the writer have?

- What does God provide when we trust Him?

drawing closer to God

For since the creation of the world God's invisible qualities—his eternal power and divine nature—have been clearly seen, being understood from what has been made, so that men are without excuse.
Romans 1:20

The Almighty God has chosen to reveal Himself to us through nature. Even so, we don't always see Him. Throughout the centuries people have tried to discover if god(s) exists and if so, in what form. For ages people have tried to put together the cosmic puzzle without knowing how. This cosmic challenge is the God-puzzle. God has given us the pieces, but we don't always put them together correctly.

To further complicate the process, Satan, the enemy of our souls, has secretly slipped extra pieces into the puzzle box. These spare pieces glitter and shine and fascinate. But whenever someone tries to use one of these pieces, it completely distorts the true picture of God. Too often the picture that results is so gruesome that the puzzle-worker rejects such a god. Or the picture shows another alluring something, something that keeps the person away from the true God. The puzzle-worker has been tricked into thinking he solved the puzzle, when in fact what he believes in is not God at all.

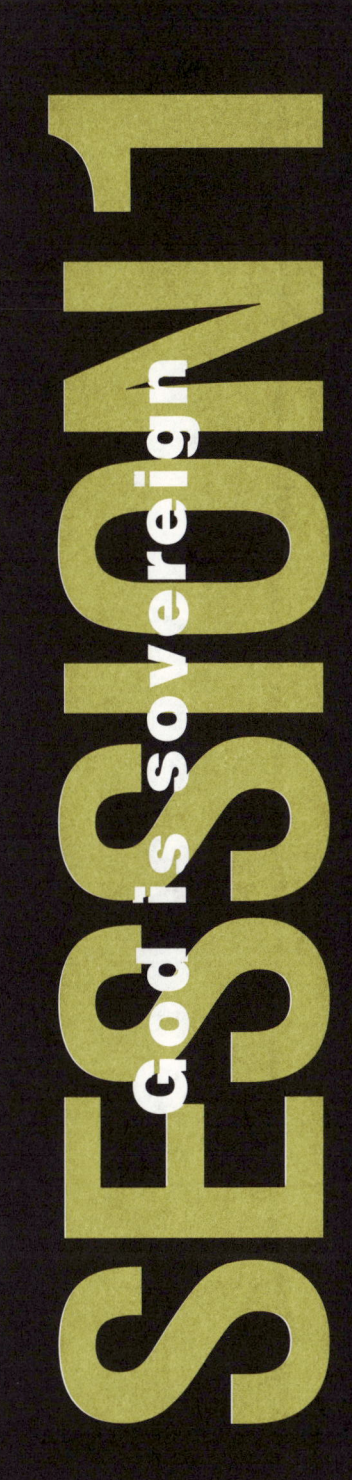

The Romans and Greeks created gods that were simply oversized editions of themselves with larger-than-life human flaws. Hindu cultures pay homage to over three million deities. Other cultures pick demon-like deities that they fear rather than trust. Animistic cultures choose to worship nature. These people-created gods leave humans very unsatisfied. People continue to work to fill the void they feel, not realizing their gods are the problem. They long to make the pieces fit and to solve the puzzle. Pascal, the famous French philosopher, identified this feeling when he said: "There is a God-shaped vacuum in the heart of every man that cannot be filled by anyone except God made known through Jesus Christ." Pascal solved the God-puzzle because he knew where to find the missing pieces. He used the pieces God provided: creation, the Bible, communication with God.

How have you experienced this God-shaped empty place? Is it a feeling, a yearning, a hurting, or what? Describe or doodle it here:

Your God-shaped empty place is filled by God. The illustration at the first of this chapter is a tree (you) putting its roots deep into the soil of God as Sovereign. In each chapter we'll add a deeper level of knowing God until we understand all six levels as illustrated at the first of Session six. Describe or doodle why it is important to you that God be Sovereign (has supreme power and authority):

The Sovereign God Communicates with You

What is the true picture of God? Because nature is not enough, God also shows us what He is like through the Bible. We know the Bible is true because of historical matches, archaeological evidences, internal agreement, and steady authenticity. (See the "Reliable Bible" sidebar for more information.) As CrossSeekers, let's examine this accurate picture of God in the Bible. Let's discover not only what God is like, but also how we can have a personal relationship with Him. Let's involve ourselves in the search to solve the God-puzzle.

It is interesting that the first book of the Bible, Genesis, does not try to prove the existence of God. It states God's existence as a fact in verse 1: *"In the beginning God…."* Much later, in the New Testament, Romans 1:18-21 sheds light on why God did not try to convince us He exists. God has revealed Himself both internally through our conscience, and externally through nature. And He holds us responsible for rightly responding to that knowledge by choosing to know Him.

God shows Himself to those who truly, without any strings attached, want to know Him. Remember God said this in Jeremiah 29:13, *"You will seek me and find me when you seek me with all your heart."* Sincere seekers find God when they stop pretending. When someone refuses the idea of God, God continues to exist and communicate. People can choose not to hear, but God is still there.

Psalm 14:1 tells of a fool, who says in his heart, *"There is no God."* This fool chooses to ignore God's impact in his life, chooses not to acknowledge God, and chooses to conclude that there must be no God. This is not a mere mental exercise. This is an atheism of practice. The person acts as though God does not exist. But no matter how many people decide there is no God, God is still there.

Perhaps something horrid has happened in this atheist's life—a drunk driver has hit and killed her brother. She concludes God must have done it, and she wants nothing to do with that God. But she has put

> **How Christianity Is Unique**
> *Religion is sometimes defined as a human being's best attempt to find God, while Christianity is defined as God's best attempt to find the human being.*

the puzzle pieces together wrong. God didn't kill her brother; the drunk driver did. God sits down and weeps along with her. If she chooses to see and know the real God, the compassionate caring God who loves both her and her brother, she would no longer be an atheist.

When have you struggled with the existence of God?

What question(s) did you ask?

How did you find the answer(s)?

To whom will you go for the answers you've not yet found?

When you genuinely doubt God's existence, you do God a favor. How? Pursuing real doubt leads to real answers and to solid faith. So pursue your doubts until you discover that God is, that God cares, and that God wants to be intimately involved in your life. The evidence is there (Rom. 1:19-20). Write a response to God about this:

> **Too Deep a Discount**
>
> *The evidence of God's existence and His gift is more than compelling, but those who insist that they have no need of Him or it, will always find ways to discount the offer.*
>
> —Pascal

The Sovereign God Has Provided a Reliable Bible

If God holds you responsible for getting to know Him, He needs to communicate to you just how to do that. This would mean being capable of communicating with you in a way you can understand, in a way you can accept as from Him. Even better, what if this God loves and has all power and all knowledge including knowledge of the future? You'd want to get to know Him, to receive His communications and act upon them. Thankfully all of this is true and all of this happens. You, a finite human, can come into the presence of Almighty God. How?

THROUGH THE BIBLE.

But how do you know the Bible is really communication from God? Many holy books exist. How do we know the Bible is the one?

Let's start with the question, "Who wrote the Bible?" God commissioned both Old Testament writers (of the first thirty-nine books in the Bible) and New Testament writers (of the remaining twenty-seven books in the Bible) to write the Word of God in God's own words. As a result we find a delightful variety of styles and perspectives, all pointing to God. It's an amazing thing called internal agreement. Internal agreement is one of the strongest evidences for the reliability of the Bible.

The Bible is also about real people who made mistakes. A made-up holy book would have the characters all doing the right thing. Its heroes would be invincible and exemplary. Bible heroes are flawed people who chose to let God use them.

The Bible also has much archaeological, historical, and manuscript evidence. People who dig to see what cultures used to be like, find clues that agree with Bible descriptions. Historical events match those found in the Bible. Copies of the Bible match with accuracy that can only be attributed to God. The deviations that do exist are minor.

As CrossSeekers who desire a right relationship with God, the Bible is essential. Because the Bible is God's revelation of Himself to you, it teaches you how to love and honor God. To answer your questions about the source and accuracy of the Bible, read books listed in the sidebar. Until you know whether you believe the Bible or not, you will continue to be confused about the character of God.

Do you trust the Bible? Why or why not?

What questions do you still have about trusting the Bible?

Reliable Bible

Plenty of holy writings exist. How do we know the Bible is the one that shows us the path to God? These books help answer this question:

- Gleason L. Archer, *Encyclopedia of Bible Difficulties* (Chicago: Moody Press, 1964).
- F. F. Bruce, *New Testament History* (New York, N.Y.: Doubleday, 1971).
- Philip Wesley Comfort, ed., *The Origin of the Bible* (Wheaton, IL: Tyndale House Publishers, 1992).
- Stephen T. Davis, *The Debate About the Bible* (Philadelphia, PA: The Westminster Press, 1977).
- Harold Lindsell, *The Bible in the Balance* (Grand Rapids, MI: Zondervan, 1979).
- *The Bible: Breathed from God* (Wheaton, IL: Victor Books, 1978).
- Josh McDowell, *Evidence That Demands a Verdict* (San Bernadino: Here's Life Publishers, 1979).
- John MacArthur, Jr., *Why I Trust the Bible* (Wheaton: Victor Books, 1983).
- Charles C. Ryrie, *A Survey of Bible Doctrine* (Chicago: Moody Press, 1972).
- Clifford A. Wilson, *Rocks, Relics and Biblical Reliability* (Grand Rapids, MI: Zondervan, 1977).

[Editor's note: Most of these are not found in bookstores; however, they may be found in your university library.]

The Sovereign God Has Shown Us What He Is Like

Do you want to know God? Look at His character to see. God reveals many aspects of His character in the Scriptures. On the journey of getting to know God, focus on these ten:

1. **Creator:** The Bible declares God is responsible for the creation of everything. It also says that He keeps all things running properly. Read Genesis 1:1; Psalm 136:5-9; Isaiah 40:25-26; 45:12; Jeremiah 5:22; 10:12; 51:15-16; Daniel 5:23; Acts 17:24-26; Hebrews 1:1.

2. **Majestic:** This characteristic describes the splendor and dignity of God. Read Psalm 93:1; 96:6; 104:1; 145:5; Isaiah 2:10, 19; 24:14; Hebrews 1:3; 8:1; 2 Peter 1:16.

3. **All-powerful:** God has the ability to do anything and everything that is not contrary to His nature. Read Genesis 18:14; Psalm 33:9-11; 93:4; Isaiah 40:26; 46:10; Jeremiah 32:17; Matthew 19:26; Luke 1:37; Romans 1:19-20; Revelation 19:6.

4. **Present everywhere:** God fully fills all places of the universe at all times. Read 1 Kings 8:27; Psalm 139:3, 5, 7-12; Isaiah 66:1; Jeremiah 23:23-24; Acts 17:27-28; Ephesians 1:23.

5. **Wise:** God has all knowledge and uses it correctly and well. Read Psalm 92:5; 136 (all); Proverbs 2:6-7; Isaiah 55:8; Jeremiah 10:12; Daniel 2:20-23; Romans 11:33-34; 16:27; Ephesians 1:17; Colossians 2:1-3; James 1:5.

6. **All-knowing:** God knows all there is to understand past, present, and future, including those things that are impossible. God never learns anything new, nor has He been taught by anyone. Read Job 38:3; Psalm 33:14-15; 147:5; Proverbs 15:3; Isaiah 40:12-31; Romans 11:33-34; Hebrews 4:13; 1 John 3:20.

7. **Holy:** Holiness is complete freedom from any sin, evil, or wrong. God is pure with absolute moral perfection. Holiness is a standard set by God's own nature. The quality of holiness of God is unique to Him. The Spirit of God is called the Holy Spirit. Read Leviticus 20:26; I Samuel 2:2; Psalm 18:30; 99:9; Isaiah 6:1-5; 1 Thessalonians 4:8; 1 Peter 1:15-16; Revelation 15:4.

8. King: God is the absolute ruler of everything and everyone in the entire universe. Read Exodus 15:18; Psalm 47:2; 93:2; 1 Timothy 1:17; 6:15-16; Hebrews 1:8; Revelation 15:3.

9. Eternal: God has no beginning and no end. Read Deuteronomy 33:27; Psalm 9:7; 90:1-2; 93:2; 102:12, 24-27; Isaiah 57:15; Habakkuk 1:12; Romans 1:20; 1 Timothy 1:17; Hebrews 9:14.

10. Infinite: God is not limited by anything including time, space, or quantity. He has unlimited existence, perfection, capacity, and energy. Read 1 Kings 8:27; 2 Chronicles 6:18; Job 11:7-9; Psalm 147:5; Isaiah 40:25; 46:5, 9-10; Jeremiah 23:24; Hebrews 6:13; Revelation 1:17-18.

These characteristics are only a glimpse into the character of the Sovereign God. People respond in their own way to the attributes of God because of their own backgrounds, personalities, gifts, and experiences. You may understand an attribute of God uniquely from someone else in your study group. So share and learn from each other.

Trying to explain God is like trying to explain a kiss. You can check the dictionary definition: "A caress with the lips; a gentle touch or contact." But does that capture the essence of what a mother does when she tenderly places her lips on the forehead of her sleeping baby? Is that what the engaged couple does when they say "good night" until their next meeting?

Just as mere words cannot completely capture a kiss, we also cannot fully comprehend, explain, or define God. We can, however, know Him through experiencing His revelation of Himself to us in the Bible. As CrossSeekers, we can know God as we see His involvement in our lives. Similar to the way married couples please each other better with each kiss, we can grow closer to God with each encounter.

Next to each of the ten characteristics of God listed previously, jot down a way you've experienced it.

Why does Christianity embody the true revelation of God to the human race? Write your answer in the space provided here. (See the "How Christianity is Unique" sidebar and other content in this chapter.)

To someone who says, "Don't be so narrow-minded. God is whoever we choose to let him be," what would you say?

The Sovereign God Invites Your Faith

Faith is only as strong as the object in which it's placed. When you put your faith in God, you build on a foundation that will hold you. The Bible tells of a man named Paul whom God directed to start churches throughout Asia Minor. One occasion found Paul a prisoner on his way to stand trial before Nero in Rome. Nero was known for his hatred of Christians. Suddenly a storm arose, threatening the safety of the ship and all on board. As the raging waves engulfed them, Paul confidently stated, *"But now I urge you to keep up your courage, because not one of you will be lost; only the ship will be destroyed. Last night an angel of the God whose I am and whom I serve stood beside me and said, 'Do not be afraid, Paul. You must stand trial before Caesar; and God has graciously given you the lives of all who sail with you.' So keep up your courage, men, for I have faith in God that it will happen just as he told me"* (Acts 27:22-25).

Paul made a simple yet profound statement of faith expressing a genuine confidence in a living God: *"I have faith in God."* Paul's calmness and tranquillity in the middle of turbulence were grounded in a personal knowledge that God would go with him.

Why do you want to put your faith in God?

Why is faith more than wishful thinking? (Seek evidence throughout this chapter.)

Encourage Your Group: Actions for Group Study

1. Discuss with your group how you know that:
   - God exists.
   - God is holy, perfect, eternal, all-powerful, present everywhere.
   - He has certain requirements of us, and we have a responsibility of some kind to Him.

2. What does nature (God's creation) teach you about Him?

3. *Sovereign* expresses the absolute rulership of God above everything and everyone else. He is under no external constraints. Read these passages to discover what God's sovereignty means: Isaiah 46:5, 9, 10; 1 Tim. 6:16-17.

Based on these Bible verses, list two ways here that you could explain God's sovereignty to someone who has no experience with God.

4. As a group, discuss how CrossSeekers can hold each other accountable for working in harmony with God's sovereignty. Write three ways here.

5. Tell about a time someone you know (including you) had an inaccurate picture of God. How did you help them (or yourself) take out the wrong pieces and put in the right ones?

6. Why is this sidebar important? "Religion is sometimes defined as a human being's best attempt to find God, while Christianity is defined as God's best attempt to find the human being."

Listen to the lyrics to "Waves" on the album *Human* by Christine Glass
(Word Music, Inc. and Soverienty, 1996).

- What is the person in this song tired of demanding?

- What thing(s) can Jesus provide better than anyone?

7. Each of you name a different reason to trust the Bible's picture of God.

8. One-by-one discuss the ten attributes of God under "The Sovereign God Has Shown Us What He Is Like." Read the verses that apply to each attribute of God.

Discuss these questions for each attribute:
    a. Why is this an important characteristic of God?
    b. What if this characteristic were not true of God?
    c. Are there any changes you should make in your life because of this truth?
    d. Where have you observed this characteristic of God? In nature, in your life, or in others?

9. Isaiah 55:8 says God is different from us. How can we know God as He is, rather than make up a God who is like we want?

10. Write a statement of faith based on what you have discovered about God in this session.

Group leading tip: The relationships that will build in your group are one of the most exciting things about being a CrossSeekers leader. Help build relationships by:
    a. Maintaining an atmosphere of warmth and positiveness.
    b. Drawing everyone into the group with an "everyone participates" rule; this keeps people from having to volunteer.
    c. Be honest and real with the members of your small group. As you open yourself up, they will feel more comfortable and participate more freely.

Between You and God

1. What do you understand about God from what He has made?

2. When have you put the puzzle pieces together to give an accurate picture of God? An inaccurate one? Think of a time for each, and explain in the space provided here.

3. How have you experienced the God-shaped empty place? How has God filled it for you?

4. Why do you trust the Bible?

5. Pick your favorite Bible verse(s) for each of the ten characteristics of God under "The Sovereign God Has Shown Us What He Is Like." Write them here.

6. Respond to, "Don't be so narrow-minded. God is whoever we choose to let him be."

7. How is faith different from wishful thinking?

   From self-fulfilling prophecy?

8. Write your own personal statement of faith to share with your group.

9. Memorize Romans 1:19-20.

10. To prepare for the next study, complete this personal evaluation: On a scale of 1-10 with 10 being total and 1 being not-at-all, rate yourself on each of these commitment areas:

    [ ] I am curious about God.
    [ ] I am certain God exists.
    [ ] I have a sense of awe toward God.
    [ ] I acknowledge the authority of God in my life.
    [ ] I am seeking the truth about God and His existence.
    [ ] I want a relationship with God.
    [ ] When I pray, my prayers are usually not centered on my needs and desires.

High numbers on the above seven show you are ready to move to the next level of intimacy with God. Feel free to talk with your group about what rankings you gave yourself.

drawing closer to God

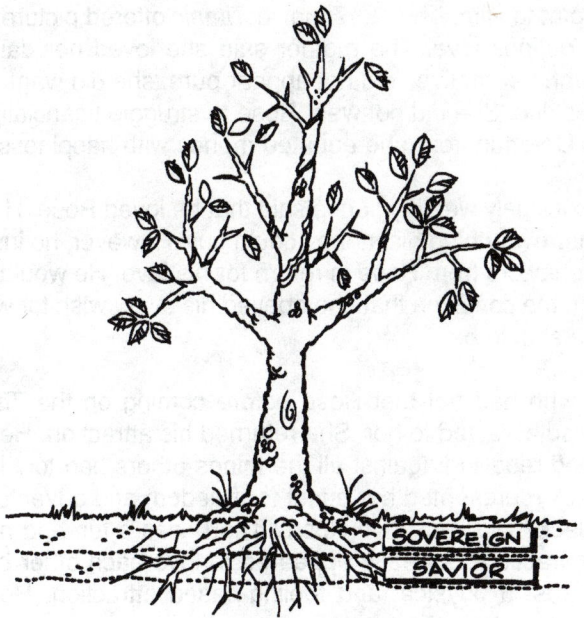

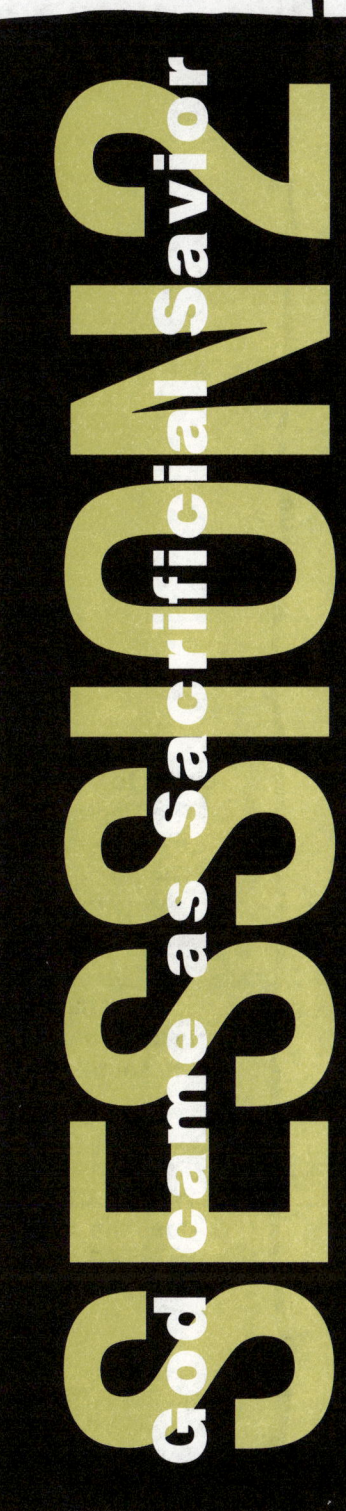

For God so loved the world that he gave his one and only Son, that whoever believes in him shall not perish but have eternal life. John 3:16

You've planted your life in the soil of the Living God. You have accepted God as Sovereign. Your seed has germinated and new life has begun. The soil is fertile and your roots are pushing deeper. You grow in the knowledge of Christ as your Savior. At this level of intimacy with God, you discover and observe new qualities about Him. God is:

- GOOD,
- LOVING,
- CARING,
- MERCIFUL,
- SACRIFICIAL,
- FORGIVING,
- ACCEPTING,
- MEDIATOR, AND
- GENTLE.

Thankfulness and gratitude for these wonderful qualities become your motivation to follow God. Your new life blossoms, because you are loved.

Though no picture from the world can fully show God's love, pictures can point to Him. The 1997 movie *Titanic* offered pictures of ways the world defines love. The mother said she loved her daughter, Rose. Although her motives did not appear pure, she did want Rose to have the best life. She did not want Rose to struggle financially, as she had done. Unfortunately, she equated money with happiness.

The extremely wealthy fiancé said that he loved Rose. He promised to give her everything his money could buy. However, he insisted on certain behaviors from Rose in return for his love. He would give his love only on the condition that she obeyed his every wish for what the proper wife should be.

Jack, who had not met Rose before coming on the *Titanic* voyage, was also attracted to her. She returned his attraction. Her love for him included rebellion against all the things others had told her to be and do. Jack represented her quest for freedom and adventure. Did Rose love Jack? Did Jack love Rose? There was a fun and naturalness to their attraction. But each appeared to love each other by the world's standards, a physical and feeling-based attraction. How could true love grow in four short days?

Finally, even if the writer did not intend it, Jack showed a glimpse of what God's love is like. Near the end of the movie, Jack did everything possible to help Rose survive the sinking of the *Titanic*. Jack even sacrificed his own life by giving Rose the piece of board floating in the ocean so Rose would not freeze in the icy waters. When Jack died, he offered a glimpse of the sacrificial love that God has for us and wants us to have for one another.

God came in the person of Jesus and died for us. He sacrificed for you and for me. How is His love deeper, wider, and truer than human love?

God the Savior Is Love

"God is love," declares John, the friend and disciple of Jesus (1 John 4:16). Human examples of love only approximate the infinitesimal love of the Almighty God for each of us humans. He loved us so much that He came to live on earth in Jesus Christ, went through everything humans go through, obeyed His own rules, and then died so we could live. We see this great love of God throughout the Scriptures. His love is unchanging, unending, and unconditional. In Jeremiah 31:3 He says, *"I have loved you with an everlasting love; I have drawn you with loving-kindness."*

Listen to the words to "The Depth of God's Love" on the album *The Basic Stuff* by Billy Crockett
(Urgent Records, 1989).

• How has God reached down to us with sacrificial love?

• What "earthy ways" does the song say express God's love?

God initiates love. He loves us first and we have the privilege of responding to His love. Isaiah presented a beautiful picture of how the God of the universe longs to have us in His presence. The passage described God sitting on His throne, as though looking out over the crowd for us. When He sees us, He rises to greet us—a sign of great honor. *"Yet the Lord longs to be gracious to you; he rises to show you compassion* (Isa. 30:18a).

What an awesome thought! The great God who has the whole universe to attend to not only knows you exist, but He looks for you and honors you when He sees you.

You may be saying, "This may be true for some people, but not for me. You don't know all the things I've done and been. God might accept me, but He surely would not long to be with me."

But it's true. God's love makes it possible. Anyone who has ever lived has sinned enough to stay permanently separated from God. In fact, God Himself knew we could never come into His presence through our own efforts. So He came to us to show us His love. John 3:16 says, *"For God so loved the world that he gave his one and only Son, that whoever believes in him shall not perish but have eternal life."*

How do you respond to a God who waits in eager anticipation to be with you?

When do you take advantage of this love?

The Savior Loves You, Warts and All

You may feel you need to clean up your life before coming to God. You may believe you must do good works or otherwise earn the right to be with Him. This would be like taking a filthy rag and trying to clean a muddy windshield. You just don't have the stuff to produce cleanliness. So Jesus died for you, even though you're a sinner. He paid for all our sins, from the time of our birth until our last breath on earth. When you accept the free gift of salvation that is offered through Jesus Christ, He can begin the cleaning process from the inside out.

> **Your Identity**
>
> *"Define yourself radically as one beloved by God.* God's love for you and his choice of you constitute your worth. Accept that, and let it become the most important thing in your life."
>
> —Brennan Manning[1]

God the Savior's love for you is based on His qualities, not yours. Notice why as you examine these two qualities of God:

1. God the Savior is Sacrificial—God freely chose to come and die, because of the great love and value He places on Humans. How could God become human and die? Because God expresses Himself in three forms: God the Father, God the Son, and God the Holy Spirit. God the Father and God the Holy Spirit allowed God the Son to become a human to live a perfect life on earth. This accomplished two purposes: (1) He could show us how to live, and (2) He could substitute for us in death. His sacrificial death, burial, and resurrection paid for the sin of each of us. Read Isaiah 53:4-7; Luke 9:20-22; John 1:1-5, 14; 3:16; Romans 3:25; Ephesians 2:4-10; Philippians 2:6-9; 1 Peter 1:18-21; 3:18.

2. God the Savior is Forgiving—To forgive is to pardon completely and give up the right to punish for sin, to never bring up the offenses again. God gave Himself in Jesus to build a bridge from Himself to us, a bridge that spans the chasm between us. When a sinner accepts Jesus' gift, he or she is free to accept God's forgiveness. Read Exodus 34:6-7; Numbers 14:18; Psalm 32:1-5; 51 (all); 86:5, 15; 103:3-4; Isaiah 1:18; 43:25; Ephesians 1:7-8; 1 John 1:9.

Have you hesitated to come into the presence of the Holy God? Explain.

How does God's sacrificial nature make you more willing to come into His presence?

How does God's forgiving nature make you more willing to let Him guide you day by day?

The Savior Is Both God and Human

God chose to become human in the person of Jesus while still maintaining His deity (his God-ness). Because He was human, He could honestly live a fully perfect life; He could be our example for daily living. His choices to do the right thing showed that we could do this as well. This is an amazing demonstration of love!

When Jesus lived on earth, He was also fully God. He claimed to be God in John 14:6-7 and in many other passages. He said, *"I am the way and the truth and the life. No one comes to the Father except through me. If you really knew me, you would know my Father as well."* Many people have claimed to be God, but only Jesus died and rose from death never to die again. The resurrection is the indisputable proof that Jesus is who He claimed to be—God Himself.

God has reached out to each of us in love. He has done all that it takes to secure our unending life with Him. But the final decision of one's eternal destiny rests in each individual's hands. If you or anyone else chooses not to accept God's only provision for our sins—the free gift God offers which allows us to live with Him forever—the consequences are our responsibility, not God's. God sends no one to hell. Only a personal choice does that.

> **Listen to the song "God So Loved" on the album *Jaci Velasquez* by Jaci Velasquez**
> (SGO Music Pub. Ltd., 1997).
>
> • How much does God love you?
>
> • Let the truth of John 3:16 fill every part of your life.

Why do you like it that Jesus was fully human?

Why do you like it that Jesus was fully God?

What are the benefits of each?

What questions do you have about each?

G.R.O.W.T.H. Acrostic

Getting to know God your Savior is an adventure. Here is an acrostic used by Campus Crusade:

Go to God daily in prayer—this is simply talking and listening to God.

Read God's Word—this is the Bible, God's instruction manual and love letter to us.

Obey what he shows us to do—Not 50%, 75%, or even 99%, but 100% obedience to God.

Witness to others what Jesus has done for you—you're always a witness; deliberately be a good one.

Trust God with every aspect of life—believe what God says and apply it to every situation you face.

Holy Spirit guides and directs our lives—Let God the Holy Spirit live in you and guide you.

God the Savior Wants You to Know Him

An important part of growing in your relationship with your Sacrificial Savior is spending time with Him. Quiet times are one way to do this. A quiet time is a time when you and God are alone together. Many people choose to spend quiet time for a few minutes at the first of each day. Others choose it as the first assignment of their homework. During a quiet time, invite God to teach you, read your Bible for a few minutes, and then talk and listen to God for a few minutes. Many quiet time guides are available to take you through Scripture in a systematic way.

You may want to keep a journal of your quiet times. This helps you remember all the Lord has done and is doing in your life. Write new things you learn about God, yourself, or others. Write questions you have about God, the Bible, and life. Write prayers you pray and answers you receive. Write special promises or things to work on in your walk with the Lord.

During the prayer portion of your quiet time:
- Express your love for God.
- Thank God for your relationship with Him.
- Thank God for what He is teaching you about Himself.
- Praise and worship God through songs and words.
- Be aware of enemy temptations and invite God's strategies to resist them.
- When problems come and you feel depressed or discouraged, remind yourself God loves you and you are special to Him. Remind yourself God will show you how to manage the

situations you face. Remember God will never leave you, as promised in Romans 8:28, 38-39.
- Thank God for His solutions to problems (1 Thess. 5:18).

The amazing part about serving a God who gave Himself for us is that He continues to give Himself to us in God the Holy Spirit. Through the Spirit, God personally dwells in each of us. He lets you take your quiet time into the rest of your day. Your quiet time then becomes the spark that gets your devotion burning throughout your whole day. What fuel is to a car, the Holy Spirit is to you, the believer. He motivates you no matter what the obstacle. He comforts you in distress, calms you in times of calamity, becomes your companion in loneliness and grief, spurs you into action, and fills your mind with discernment when you need to make a decision. He is your spiritual fuel. Attempting to work without Him means you will grind to a halt.

What has been your greatest frustration in having a quiet time?

What has been your greatest joy in having a quiet time?

What amazes you about a God who saves you and then dwells within you?

Encourage Your Group: Actions for Group Study

1. What human examples have you seen that hint at the way God loves?

2. What have you learned about love directly from God?

3. How is your love life different now that you realize God's great love for you? Give an example in friendships, study habits, and guy/girl relationships.

Your Heart's True Home

"Today the heart of God is an open wound of love. He aches over our distance and preoccupation. He mourns that we do not draw near to him. He grieves that we have forgotten him. He weeps over our obsession with muchness and manyness. He longs for our presence."
—Richard J. Foster[2]

4. Take turns answering these questions until each member of your group has given a different answer for each question. Jot down each member's answers so you have a broad understanding of God as Savior:

   • Who is Jesus?

   • What is His relationship to God?

   • What type of person was He?

   • Why did He come to live on earth?

   • What keeps you from spending time with Jesus your Sacrificial Savior?

5. Using what you just discovered, how would you describe God as Savior without any churchy words?

6. What growth have you seen in your spirituality from the time you first knew God existed until this day?

7. Reread Jeremiah 31:3. What do you like about the word loving-kindness? What other two words would you put together to describe God's love? Each member choose different ones.

8. How do you describe God as both divine and human?

9. What one tip would you offer someone for a good quiet time habit?

10. How can we as CrossSeekers hold each other accountable to follow the Holy Spirit's leadership?

Group Leading Tip: Help the group become comfortable with one another by doing something together outside your meeting time. Perhaps you can share one meal in the cafeteria weekly.

Between You and God

1. What difference does it make that God greatly loves you and cares about everything that happens to you?

2. Why would you recommend someone accept God as Savior? Name at least five reasons.

3. What responses do each of these characteristics of God elicit in you?

- God is good:

- God is loving:

- God is caring:

- God is merciful:

- God is sacrificial:

- God is forgiving:

- God is accepting:

- God is mediator:

- God is gentle:

4. What Bible verse most powerfully reminds you of God's love, and why? (Samples include Isa. 30:18, John 3:16, and 1 John 1:5.)

5. Are you likely to take God's sacrifice and forgiveness too lightly, or too heavily?

   How does God want you to weigh them just right?

6. Answer the questions at the end of "The Savior Wants You to Know Him."

7. To discover just what God in Jesus Christ is like, read the Gospel of John. As you read the book, record answers to these questions:

   • Who is Jesus?

   • What type of person was He?

   • Why did He come to live on earth?

8. What one change will you make in your quiet time? What one thing will you keep the same?

9. Complete this personal evaluation before moving to the next chapter: On a scale of 1-10 with 10 being total and 1 being not-at-all, rate yourself on where you are in each of these commitment areas:
   - [ ] I see God as a personal God, not just a God who started everything and left us to our ways.
   - [ ] I have some trust in God.
   - [ ] I am thankful to God for all He has done for me.
   - [ ] Sometimes I feel overwhelmed by my relationship with God.
   - [ ] I have invited Jesus into my life as my Savior and as the Lord of my life.

- [ ] I have an inner desire to obey God, even if I do not always succeed in doing so.
- [ ] I am aware of areas of my life that are not pleasing to God.
- [ ] I read the Bible and pray.
- [ ] I allow the Holy Spirit to control my actions.
- [ ] I am, or have been, excited about my relationship with God.

As you incorporate the above areas into your life, you grow ready to move to the next level.

10. To prepare for the next study, ponder why God is a good father.

Notes

[1] Brennan Manning, *Abba's Child: The Cry of the Heart for Intimate Belonging* (Colorado Springs: NavPress, 1994) 49. Used by permission of NavPress Publishing. All rights reserved. For copies of the book, call 800-366-7788.

[2] Richard J. Foster, *Prayer: Finding the Heart's True Home* (San Francisco, CA: Harper, 1992) 1.

drawing closer to God

I will be a Father to you, and you will be my sons and daughters, says the Lord Almighty. 2 Corinthians 6:18

Now that you have the foundation of salvation, you can go deeper and wider into what can become the closest of relationships with God. When Jesus Christ walked this planet, He pushed aside the typical pictures of the Almighty to show us a previously unrecognized picture—God wants to be our Daddy. Have you found this piece of the God-puzzle in your life?

God is not an impersonal force ruling creation. He is not a tyrant sitting in the clouds waiting for any opportunity to ruin your personal goals and dreams. He actually cares about what is going on down here. In fact, Jesus described God with two simple, yet profound, words: Our Father. As Jesus taught His disciples how to pray, He said, "This, then, is how you should pray: *'Our Father in heaven, hallowed be your name'"* (Matt. 6:9).

God wants you to grow your relationship with Him by thinking of Him as your Father. There are over seventy references to the paternal nature of God in the New Testament. God wants you to relate to Him as Father, not as some mystical influence in the universe.

For some, the word *father* brings images of someone who loves you no matter what, someone whose lap you loved and whose tickles you cherished. For others the word *father* may bring to the surface fear, resentment, and even guilt. As a child you may have heard, "You just

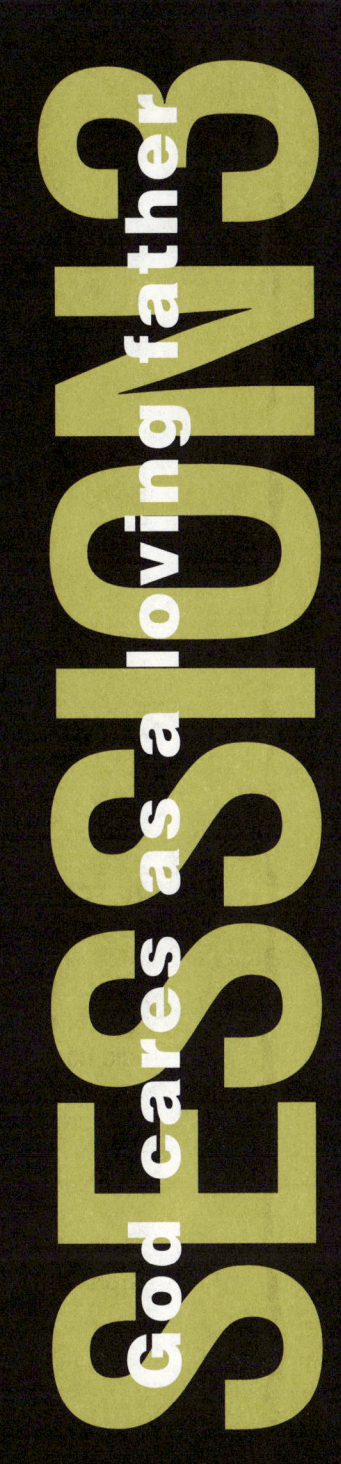

wait until your father gets home." Then you went to church, and heard, "God is our Father." Very subtly, you began to view God as the one who would punish you when He got close. Perhaps Jesus knew about these mixed experiences. Maybe that's why He clarified the title by saying, "Our Father *in heaven.*"

"Heaven" has little to do with location, but more to do with a state of perfection. No earthly father is as good as God. But God our Father in heaven is perfect. He relates to you as a perfectly caring father. A good earthly father imitates God. But a bad earthly father does not change the goodness of your Heavenly Father.

What does God teach you about how a father should be?

Guys, how will this influence the father you become? Gals, how will this influence the one you choose to marry and become the father of your children?

Status Changes as Believers

After you trust God as your Savior, you have a reconciled-to-God status. You become a child of God. Look at the wonderful ways the Bible describes this:

BEFORE SALVATION	AFTER TRUSTING CHRIST
"Enemies" (Rom. 5:8-11)	"Sons" or "children" (John 1:12, Gal. 4:7, 1 John 3:1)
"Slaves" (Gal. 4:1-8) who "did not know God"	"Adopted" children who call God "Abba, Father" with full rights (Rom. 8:15-17, Gal. 4:5-7)
"Children of wrath" (Eph. 2:3)	"Children of light" (John 12:36, Eph. 5:8)
"Foreigners and aliens" (Eph. 2:19)	"Members of God's household" (Eph. 2:19)
"Sons and daughters of disobedience" (Eph. 2:2)	"Sons and daughters" of the Father (2 Cor. 6:18)

Your God Is a Compassionate Father

What kind of Father is our God in heaven? **First, God is a compassionate Father.** *"As a father has compassion on his children, so the Lord has compassion on those who fear him"* (Ps. 103:13). To have compassion means to feel with, to understand just what the other feels, and why. Does God care about your classes? Yes! Does He care about your checkbook that never seems to balance? Yes! Does He care what friends you pick and how those friends treat you? Yes! Does He care about that relationship that has never become what you hoped it would? Yes! He cares about everything in your life. Remember the promise in 1 Peter 5:7, *"Cast all your anxiety on him because he cares for you."*

What feelings do you regularly share with God?

What other feelings would He like you to talk with Him about?

Why do you agree or disagree with the "Roots of Love" sidebar?

> **The Roots of Love**
>
> Too often in our spiritual life—although we may need to love God more—there is a much higher need to recognize just how much He loves us. When our relationship is such that we feel God's love and His passion for His children, we naturally begin to love Him more.

Your God Is a Persistent Father

Second, God is a persistent Father. You can always count on Him. Because He never changes, He is worthy of your trust. Earthly fathers can be unpredictable, as can any human being. Some people will tell you, "I just don't know what to expect from my dad. One minute he lets me have my own way; the next he's a dictator. I can't figure him out." The result of this kind of inconsistency is insecurity. But God is consistent. You can find security in Him.

God does not have good days and bad days. Because of His grace, He loves you persistently on your good and bad days. His nature is revealed in 2 Timothy 2:13, *"If we are faithless, he will remain faithful, for he cannot disown himself."* Isn't that incredible? Even when you struggle, even when you are faithless and filled with doubt, God is persistent. Despite the fact that everything else around you may change, and your world may fall apart, there is always one thing you can count on: God continues to love you.

God's refusal to change has great advantages. Name some of these.

God's refusal to change has what some would call disadvantages—you can't manipulate Him, or get Him to cover up wrong for you. Why do you like even these "disadvantages?"

Your God Is a Personal Father

Third, God is a personal Father. He always has time for each of His children. You are not more or less important than any other believer. He is never too busy for you. You don't have to stand in line or wait your turn. Psalm 145:18 tells us, *"The Lord is near to all who call on him, to all who call on him in truth."* When you pray, you will never get a busy signal. He is never more concerned about a crisis in the Middle East than He is with your individual problem. Your heavenly Father has unlimited resources. He is not limited by time, space, or energy. Your God is a personal, loving Father. He is sympathetic to your hurts. He understands. Really. In fact, He's been through everything you have (Heb. 2:17-18; 4:15-16). There's no need to hide anything from God. Psalm 34:18 states, *"The Lord is close to the brokenhearted and saves those who are crushed in spirit."* Have you had a tough week, a tough year, or even a tough life? God is near. Have you had a great week, a great year, a great life? God is near. He can help with both.

Jesus used a very special term to describe the personal nature of God. He called Him, *"Abba."* Abba is an Aramaic word for the most intimate, personal nature of a father. We use the word *Daddy.* God wants us to enjoy this type of closeness, because He is a personal Father.

Name three things you enjoy about God being your daddy.

What is your favorite verse about God being close to you?

The Names for God

God's names are more than labels. They reveal His nature and character. The Bible records several names for God. Each represents a different attribute. Together they provide a complete picture of God. Here is a sample of the many names of God:

Yahweh-Roi	"The Lord, my Shepherd"
Yahweh-Jireh	"The Lord shall provide"
Yahweh-Shalom	"The Lord our peace"
Yahweh-Rophe	"The Lord our healer"
Yahweh-Tsidkenu	"The Lord our righteousness"
Yahweh-Nissi	"The Lord my banner"
Yahweh-Shammah	"The Lord is there"
Yahweh-Mekaddishkhem	"The Lord that sanctifies you"
El Shaddai	"The God who supplies my needs"
El Elyon	"Possessor of heaven and earth"
El Olam	"The everlasting God"
El Gibbor	"The mighty God"
Yahweh-Melek	"The God who is King"
Yahweh-Sabaoth	"The Lord of hosts"
Adonai	"The Lord/Master"
Elohim	"God"
Yahweh	"Lord"
Pater	"Father"

Your God Is a Prepared Father

Fourth, God is a prepared Father. Nothing surprises God because He can handle every situation. We have limitations, but God does not. Ephesians 3:20 tells us, *"Now to him who is able to do immeasurably more than all we ask or imagine, according to his power that is at work within us."* Our heavenly Father has unlimited knowledge, resources, and power. He frequently meets our needs Himself. Other times He provides a parent, friend, boyfriend or girlfriend, boss, professor or other person. These people cannot meet our needs on their own. They can do it only with God as their source.

What makes it easy for you to trust God to meet your needs?

When have you tried to work in competition with His plan?

Your God Is a Permanent Father

Fifth, God is a permanent Father. Approximately four thousand years ago our loving God guided His children out of Egypt. They came to the Red Sea, and God parted the waters. The people of Israel were deeply thankful that God had been so faithful to them.

But three days later, they complained and questioned the things God had displayed to them just a few miles back. You have likely responded in the same way. You have seen God's faithfulness in your life, yet you later questioned whether God would work again. Has God changed? Nope. He's the same yesterday, today, and forever. God cares for you, and always will.

Why do people tend to blame God when things go wrong, but credit themselves when things go right?

Isn't it more likely that the wrongs are our doing and the rights are God's doing?

Your God Wants You to Refine Your Image of Him

So what do you do when you have a distorted father image? You deliberately redraw the image to match God's picture. You refuse to allow earthly hurts from parents or others in authority to distort your understanding of God. You invite God to heal the feelings, fears, and human experiences that threaten to block a clear perception of God.

Somewhere along the way you may have learned a distorted picture of God the Father. Don't panic. God will help you. Your hesitancy to trust God may have been created by someone in a position of authority over you. Distinguish these people from God. No matter how badly they have treated you, God can heal that. No matter how well they have treated you, God is even better. Likely your parents have been good at some things and not so good at others. Redraw your image of God so it matches God, not people.

What marks does God want you to erase on your picture of Him?

What accurate marks will make your picture match who He really is?

Your God Wants to Be Your Daddy

Remember the story of Pinocchio—the wooden puppet who wanted to become a real boy? At times we are like Pinocchio, wanting to become real children of God, but choosing to stubbornly listen to the advice of other boys rather than the father who loves us. Like Pinocchio we can focus on human ways and advice, or we can learn directly from our daddy.

Pinocchio's story is like the prodigal son, with a touch of Jonah and the whale. Psalm 32:9 says, *"Do not be like the horse or the mule, which have no understanding but must be controlled by bit and bridle or they will not come to you."*

Rather than turn mule-ish, turn your stubbornness into determination to know and love God as Father. Stubbornly discover what you can do to please God. Keep seeking while He continues to show you how to please Him. Allow God's Holy Spirit to give you His power and ability to do these things. Perhaps God wants you to be more loving, or more in control of anger, less afraid, more trusting, kinder, or more patient. What does God expect of His children? Here are five examples:

1. Honor	*"If I am a father, where is the honor due me?"* (Mal. 1:6).	
	Read also: Psalm 45:6; Proverbs 3:9; John 5:23	
2. Obey	*"If anyone loves me, he will obey my teaching"* (John 14:23).	
	Read also: 1 Samuel 15:22; Psalm 119:34, 67; Jeremiah 7:23, 11:4;	
3. Love	*"Love the Lord your God with all your heart"* (Deut. 6:5).	
	Read also: Psalm 31:23; John 14:23-24, 15:9-11	
4. Please	*"Live in order to please God"* (1 Thess. 4:1).	
	Read also: Romans 12:1; 2 Corinthians 5:9; Hebrews 11:6, 13:21	
5. Imitate	*"Be imitators of God"* (Eph. 5:1).	
	Read also: Matthew 5:48; 1 Thessalonians 1:6; 1 John 1:7	

Read 1 Corinthians 13 on love. How does God want you to improve your love life in the above five ways? (Hint: Love includes both the way we treat God, and the way we treat people because we love God.)

Encourage Your Group: Actions for Group Study

1. How is your father like God? How is your father different from God? How does God teach you to be a better father or mother, one day?

2. How do you know God is compassionate?

3. We talk a lot about bad fathers. Describe a man you know who shows consistent love similar to God's consistency.

   What action can you take to grow like this man?

4. In what area will you persist, similar to the way God persists? (school work; building friendships; other)

5. What makes you think you are better or worse than another Christian? How will you let God relate to YOU, not "better than" or "worse than"?

6. Each of you choose a name for God and draw or describe for the group what it teaches you about God.

7. What's the cure for whining to God? (See "Your God Is a Permanent Father.")

8. Which of the distorted father-image characters (under "Your God Wants You to Refine Your Image of Him") do you relate to most strongly? What lines will you erase and what lines will you draw in to show a more accurate picture of God our Father?

9. Each of you choose one love-your-Heavenly-Father action: honor, obey, love, please, imitate. Prepare a 60-second speech on why this is important.

10. How can we as CrossSeekers encourage each other to rightly relate to God as Father?

Group leading tip: Remember that each individual will be at a different place in their spiritual walk. As the leader, affirm EACH member of your group as he or she participates in discussions. Notice the gift that each member shows—one may show mercy while another shows prophecy. Show the group how to encourage each member with a rule that everyone speaks before any speaks a second time—then each will grow to anticipate what the other contributes.

Between You and God

1. Read 2 Corinthians 6:18. Snuggle up in God's lap for a time of prayer with Him.

2. What is God teaching you about what the relationship *father* really means?

3. Do you need to give more attention to letting God love you, or letting you love God?

4. Your God is compassionate. For each feeling, write a sentence to tell God about it:

    - confusion

    - fear

    - excitement

    - anger

    - anticipation

    - discovery

    - more: _____

5. Read 2 Timothy 2:13. What actions and attitudes on your part would lead God to say this about you?

6. Almighty God can give attention to every believer whenever he or she needs Him. How do you suppose He does this?

7. Recall a time God has outdone what you asked Him to do (Eph. 3:20).

8. What caricature of God as Father most distorts your image of Him? How will you refocus the picture?

9. How will you become God's teachable child rather than a mulish rebel? Read 1 John for ideas. Memorize 1 John 1:5.

10. Personal evaluation: On a scale of 1-10 with 10 being total and 1 being not-at-all, rate yourself on where you are in each of the following commitment areas:

    [ ] I have a strong sense of being a loved child of God.
    [ ] I am convinced God is on my side.
    [ ] I try to obey God's Word.
    [ ] I pray.
    [ ] I trust God in most things.
    [ ] God is helping me develop more self-control in difficult situations.
    [ ] I am worthy because God loves me.
    [ ] I see God as a good, kind, and loving Father whom I can trust.

Most of your rankings should be above five to move to the next level.

11. To prepare for the next study, read Micah 6:8 and ponder how God's constant companionship will help you do this.

Steps To Forgiving a Dad

A dad or another authority figure may have treated you in a way that makes it hard to trust God the Father. How can you forgive that person and move on to a healthy relationship with God?

1. Acknowledge the hurt and the hate you may have. Talk with God about how this person has hurt you. Tell God about the bitterness or hatred you have for this person because of what they did to you. This is where the healing begins. Forgiveness lets you face your pain and leave the other person to God.
2. Decide you will forgive this person and not use this situation against him or her in the future. You can choose to quit the hate and bitterness, and directly fix the consequences. You will live with the consequences of that person's sin whether you want to or not. However, you can choose whether you will do so in the bitterness of unforgiveness, or the freedom of forgiveness.
3. Make the choice to forgive now. Don't wait until you feel like forgiving the person. Forgiveness is a head thing, not a feeling thing. You don't have to forget to forgive. You don't have to feel like forgiving. You just have to choose to forgive. The feelings will take time to heal after the choice to forgive is made. You don't forgive someone for his or her sake; you do it for you. You need to forgive so you can be free.
4. Ask God to help you forgive. Here's a sample: "God, I have been hurt by _____. It is hard to forgive him/her but I know You want me to do so. Therefore I choose, as an act of my will to forgive _____ and let it no longer interfere with my freedom in You."

How can you tell if you have trouble relating to God the Father? Check yes or no beside each of these questions:
- Do you find it easier to relate to Jesus than to the Father? __ yes __ no
- Do you inwardly bristle when told to do something? __ yes __ no
- Are you afraid God will ask you to do something too hard for you? __ yes __ no
- Are you afraid you may have to give up something if you tell God He can have His way in your life? __ yes __ no
- Do you sometimes feel God is sitting up in heaven, just waiting for you to make a mistake? __ yes __ no
- Are there things you don't want God to ask you to do because you just don't want to do them? __ yes __ no
- Do you feel God is disappointed in you, or not pleased with you? __ yes __ no

- Do you feel God wants you to do or not to do certain things to get His goals accomplished—despite how you feel? __ yes __no
- Do you avoid reading certain verses in the Bible because you know you don't live up to them? __ yes __no
- Do you see God as someone too busy running the universe to bother with your small problems? __ yes __no
- Are you afraid to ask God for certain things because you are sure He will say no? __ yes __no
- Do you feel uncertain of your relationship with the Father—that you may do something that will disqualify you from heaven? __ yes __no

If you answered yes to any of the previous questions, you probably need to repair your view of God.

drawing closer to God

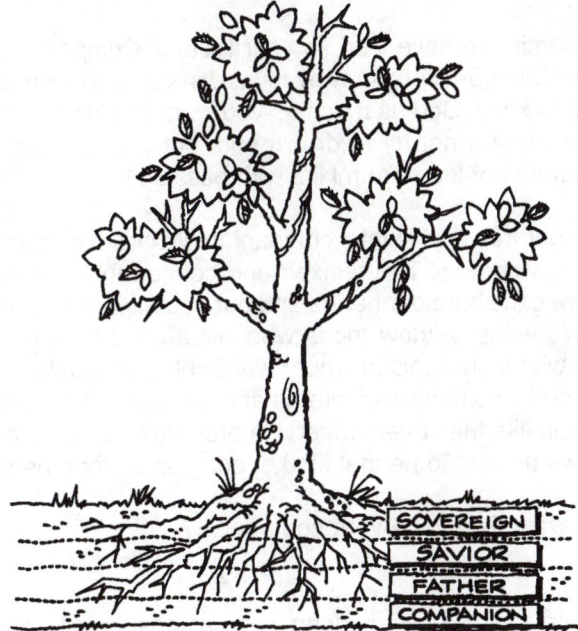

And what does the Lord require of you? To act justly and to love mercy and to walk humbly with your God. Micah 6:8

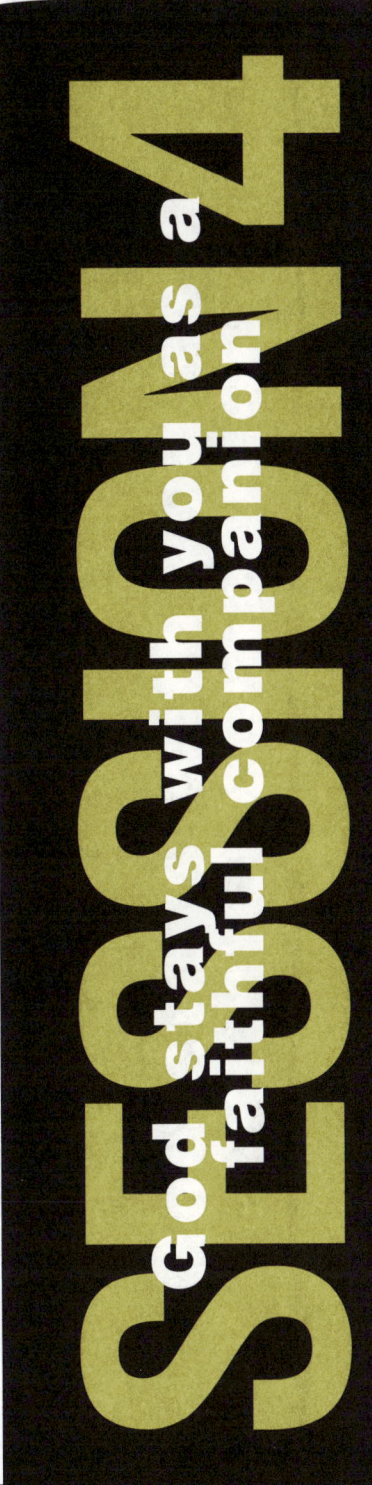

SESSION 4
God stays with you as a faithful companion

There is a wonderful story of a young man who sought out a wise, old philosopher. The young man wanted to learn from the sage. When he found the old man sitting by a lake, he asked, "Sir, I would like to sit at your feet, be your disciple, and learn wisdom from you."

The sage did not reply. Instead he stood up, approached the young man, and shoved him into the water. Then the old man jumped in on top of the boy and held his head under water. The boy was surprised and confused. Thoughts swirled in his head. This must be a joke! He will let me up in a minute.

The young man's air escaped in bubbles to the surface. His lungs screamed for oxygen. Suddenly he realized this was not a joke. Soon he was going to drown. Arms flaying, he was able to throw the old man off and surface for a gulp of air. Suddenly he was pushed down again. Fear and anger swept over him, and he threw off the old man again.

Screaming, the young man exploded, "You are crazy! I came to learn from you. I wanted to be your disciple. But you are trying to kill me!" Then the sage replied in a soft, but firm voice, "Young man, when you want to learn from me as much as you wanted to get out of the water, only then will you be ready to learn."

Are you screaming to have God as your Faithful Companion? This is the next level we CrossSeekers journey toward in our walk with Jesus Christ. Do you want to know God as much as you want to breathe? God is ready to teach you. He will not try to drown you, but you yourself will get into messes if you do not learn from Him with passion.

God will be your true and faithful companion. What's a companion? A rare individual with whom we feel relaxed and comfortable. We crave friends with whom we can share our hearts and our secrets and know they will not betray us. We want to know those who will always be there for us. We desire to be with individuals in whom we can have confidence—ones we can respect and who in turn admire us and want us to be successful. God is a companion like this. Even better, He prepares human companions for us, and shows us how to be that kind of companion for others.

Why do you want God to be your companion?

Why are people who have a deep companionship with God the best human companions for you?

"Thoughts in Solitude"

My Lord God, I have no idea where I am going. I do not see the road ahead of me. I cannot know for certain where it will end. Nor do I really know myself, and the fact that I think I am following your will does not mean that I am actually doing so. But I believe that the desire to please you does in fact please you. And I hope I have that desire in all that I am doing. I hope that I will never do anything apart from that desire. And I know that if I do this you will lead me by the right road, though I may know nothing about it. Therefore I will trust you always though I may seem to be lost and in the shadow of death. I will not fear, for you are ever with me, and you will never leave me to face my perils alone.

—Thomas Merton

What Is a Companion?

God wants to be your companion—your comfortable-to-be-with one in whom you have confidence and to whom you want to tell everything. God is even better than any earthly companion, because He has no human limitations. He knows the road you're traveling and all the joys and problems that lie ahead. He gives dependable advice. He won't put you down when you stumble. He will never desert you when you fail or don't live up to His standards. He accepts you just as you are. He wants to be with you forever. God is able to help you be all you can be. God can enable you to avoid or overcome every obstacle or problem life pitches you. Another piece of the God-puzzle!

As your Companion, God is also your Loving Father, your Sacrificial Savior, and your Holy Sovereign. All the attributes you've learned about Him till now are still true about Him, but you'll find even greater depths and aspects of these attributes as you walk further with Him at this new level. You will also discover new attributes including these eight: **Kind, Wonderful, Encouraging, Peace-giving, Counselor, Empowerer, Consistently Giving, and Trustworthy**.

- If God were not **kind**, could I trust Him when He asked me to do something?
  Thankfully, God is **kind**. He does what is right without partiality (Deut. 10:17, Isa. 61:8; Acts 10:34-35; Rom. 2:6, 11; Eph. 6:8; Heb. 6:10; 1 Pet. 1:17; Rev. 15:3).

- If God were not **full of wonder**, would I look forward to each day with as much anticipation?
  Thankfully, God is **wonderful**. He is marvelous, exceedingly good, excellent, fine, and admirable (Ex. 15:11; Ps. 33; 35:10; 71:19; 139:6; Isa. 9:6; 25:1; Matt. 21:15; Acts 2:11; Rev. 15:3).

- If God were not **encouraging** would I find it easy to trust His compassion and His solutions to my problems?
  Thankfully, God is **encouraging**. He gives support, help, and confidence (Deut. 31:6-8; Ps. 17:8; 34:18; Isa. 41:13; 2 Thess. 2:16-17).

- If God were not **peace-giving**, could I have the stability to go through happiness without getting full of myself, or go through sadness without panic? Could I manage seemingly impossible situations?
  Thankfully God not only **gives peace**, but **is peace**. He provides the absence of disorder with calm, quiet tranquillity (Ps. 29:11; 119:165; Isa. 9:6; 26:3, 12; Micah 5:5; John 14:27; 16:33; Rom. 1:7; 15:33; Gal. 5:22; Eph. 2:14; Phil. 4:6-9; Col. 3:15; 2 Thess. 3:16).

- If God were not **constant,** could I trust his **counsel**? Could He loyally keep His promises and commitments?
  Thankfully, God is **constant.** God gives the perfect guidance from a position of having all knowledge and wanting the best for us (Ps. 16:7; 23; 31:19; 32:8-9; 73:24; 89:1-2, 5, 8, 14, 24, 28, 33; 119:90; Isa. 9:6; 25:1; 46:11; Rom. 8:38-39; 1 Thess. 5:24; 2 Thess. 3:3; 2 Tim. 2:13; James 1:17; 1 John 1:9).

- If God could not **empower** me, why should I trust Him?
  Thankfully, God not only has power, but **empowers** His children. He will give you the power to live the Christian life successfully (Ps. 18:29; 119:9, Isa. 30:21; 40:29; John 16:13; 1 Cor. 10:13; Eph. 1:19; 3:20; 6:10-17; Phil. 1:6; 2:12-13: 4:13, 19; 2 Thess. 1:11; 2:16-17; 3:3).

- If God did not **give,** how would I learn generosity? How would I have His resources to share?
  Thankfully, God does **give.** He provides whatever we need, through showing us how to find it, and through many other ways (Ps. 84:11; 119:30; Prov. 3:34-35; Isa. 40:29; Luke 11:9-10; John 3:16; Acts 11:17; Eph. 2:7; 3:20; Phil 4:19; 1 Pet. 1:4; 1 John 5:11).

- Without **trust,** how secure would I feel in doing what God asks?
  Thankfully, God is **trustworthy.** He is worthy of our confidence because He is honest, dependable, and faithful, with integrity (Ps. 4:5; 9:10; 25:9-10; 27:13; 37:3-5; 52:8; 56:3-11; 111:7; 138:8; Jer. 29:11-14; Lam. 3:22-23; 1 Cor. 10:13; Heb. 2:13; 1 John 1:5).

Why do you value each of these eight attributes of God?

How Does Companionship Make You Want God's Will?

Companionship brings out a mutuality that is delightful. Because God cares for you, you want to care for Him. Because God understands you, you want to understand Him. Because God trusts you, you want to trust Him. You do all this obeying and delighting in Him. You want to understand and do His will.

To live in the center of God's will and experience His companionship is the greatest thing that can happen to you. Romans 12:1-2 says, *"Therefore, I urge you, brothers, in view of God's mercy, to offer your* bodies as living sacrifices, holy and pleasing to God—this is your spiritual act of worship. Do not conform any longer to the pattern of this world, but be transformed by the renewing of your mind. Then you will be able to test and approve what God's will is—his good, pleasing and perfect will."

How has God been your companion today?

How have you done His will as a result?

Have you discovered another piece of the God-puzzle?

What Critical Hindrance Will You Remove?

A huge hindrance threatens your companionship with God—your desire to be independent. You may not want anyone—even God—to tell you what to do. This is normal, but super-dangerous! The devil will jump right on this and let your self-centeredness keep you separated from God. He'll stoke your mistrust to keep you from discovering that true freedom comes from willing obedience.

So push Satan aside like the nuisance he is. Choose to embrace God as Faithful Companion. Until now, your obedience may have been based on fear or another selfish motive. Now choose to obey Him out of love. Why? As you realize how good God truly is and how much He loves you, you realize you'd be a fool not to obey Him. As a CrossSeeker, grow free to experience His love in a deeper way.

Now that God is your companion, why do you want to obey?

How will your obedience give you more independence than you give up?

Why Does Obedience Matter?

Little is more disappointing than expecting a good crisp apple and getting a mushy, bruised one. It's just not what God intends an apple to be. At the same time, we cheat ourselves when we refuse to let God's fruit grow and show in us. Galatians 5:22-23 states, *"But the fruit of the Spirit is love, joy, peace, patience, kindness, goodness, faithfulness, gentleness and self-control. Against such things there is no law."* So, how many fruits of the Spirit are there? If your answer is nine, look again. There is one—and this is very significant.

If you believe that these verses describe "fruits" of the Spirit rather than the "fruit" of the Spirit, you will pick a freedom not designed in the Bible, a freedom to be picky about the fruit you want and the behavior you desire. But when you see all nine characteristics as a single unit, you get to enjoy the crisp and all-round behavior that results from displaying all the fruit. Being rooted in your Lord and trusted Companion helps this happen. There's a connection between roots and fruit. As the roots go deeper, the fruit ripens and becomes good.

How has companionship with God already produced love, joy, peace, patience, kindness, goodness, faithfulness, gentleness, and self-control in you?

Scriptural Connection of Root and Fruit in the Eyes of Faith

Companionship with God brings forth spiritual fruit because the fruits have their origin in God:

FRUIT	**CHARACTER OF GOD (ROOT)**
Love	God is love (1 John 4:16).
Joy	He will rejoice over you (Zeph. 3:17).
Peace	He is the God of peace (Heb. 13:20-21).
Patience	He is patient with you (2 Pet. 3:9).
Kindness	He is kind (Eph. 2:7).
Goodness	I will see the goodness of the Lord (Ps. 27:13).
Faithfulness	Great is [God's] faithfulness (Lam. 3:23).
Gentleness	[Jesus is] gentle (Matt. 11:29).
Self-Control	God shows strength in all settings (Luke 1:51).

How Does Your Heart Respond to Your Companion?

A wise person once said, "When God measures you, He puts a tape around your heart, not your head." So, how is your heart doing? As one drawing closer to God, you will notice a more intense desire to please God. You deepen in your care for people.

You may still have difficulty finding time to read the Bible, but once you get started, you delight in the little discoveries you make there. A hunger for God's Word grows in you. You make daily Bible reading a priority, similar to the way you establish a habit of church attendance and daily school study. Jesus established similar habits, and is our model for doing so (Luke 4:16). Studying God's Word gives you a greater sense of His care and your security in Him.

As one drawing closer to God, you have a growing sense of God's love and acceptance. You talk to Him more regularly, even asking for guidance as you walk to class or see someone approach. As your Companion, God stays with you through good times and bad, and you stay with Him. He leads you to specific promises in the Bible that help you in each circumstance. You can almost see Him smiling at you, guiding and encouraging you in what you are doing, pleased with you. Psalm 23 describes this close companionship with God our Shepherd.

You find yourself more in love with God and more in awe of who He is. You want to please Him more and have a deeper understanding of His great love for you. Your heart and emotions may be touched at times as you think of your developing relationship with the Lord.

With God as your Faithful Companion, you become more submissive to God's will. This voluntary yielding in love grows out of a heart of joy, not obligation. You struggle less to submit to His leading because your trust in Him is growing. Your life shows His control in more areas, especially speech, temper, and actions. You have a greater ability to praise God. Praising God becomes more natural. And you learn new ways of praising Him.

As a CrossSeeker, how are you pursuing consistent spiritual growth?

Write phrases from this section to describe what is happening to you.

Why Do You Want to Please Your Companion?

Please God not to earn his companionship—you already have that—but to show Him how much His companionship means to you. Choose a situation in your life. Decide to please God in that area, to do His will. Follow these seven steps and have your group pray with you as you seek God's will on this issue. Stick with it no matter how long it takes. The wait will be worth it. Then try a new area. The adventure will go on and on.

Step 1: Pray. Remember that prayer is as much listening as talking. If you don't listen, how can God guide you?

Step 2: Commit to the importance of God's Word in your life for guidance. The Bible is unquestionably the most important avenue for evaluating your beliefs and actions. As you become attentive and open your heart to learn, God eagerly teaches you.

Step 3: Obey what God has already revealed in the Bible. This absolute prerequisite demonstrates your submission and openness to God.

Step 4: Trust the Holy Spirit's leading. He will help you obey what you already understand in the Bible as well as help you grasp new concepts. Jesus explained that the Holy Spirit is given to every believer (John 14:16-17; Rom. 8:14). The Bible commands each believer to be filled with the Holy Spirit (Eph. 5:18)—He's already inside. We just have to let Him work. Day by day He shows us how to live for God in more areas of our lives.

Step 5: Counsel with other trusted believers. Even though our primary counsel must be from God's Word, God also uses experienced believers to teach us the truth. Sometimes these believers talk to us; other times we watch their actions.

Step 6: Evaluate recent circumstances. Not everything that happens is sent to you by God. But He does provide providential circumstances to guide you and motivate you. If circumstances contradict the Bible's guidance, choose the Bible every time. A cute guy may have asked you out just as you prayed for a date, but if he doesn't walk daily with God, he's not the guy to say yes to.

Step 7: Decide and wait for God's peace. God's peace will be the stamp of approval on your decision. Uneasiness can mean the devil's input; or that you simply need to wait a little longer.

How can we CrossSeekers hold each other accountable to seek and do God's will through these seven steps?

How can we encourage each other to develop comfortable companionship with God?

Encourage Your Group: Actions for Group Study

1. How are you bored with learning from God rather than totally focused on it, like the young man screaming for air?

How can we as CrossSeekers prompt each other to yearn to learn from God?

2. Describe companionship in three words. How is God this Companion for you?

3. Take turns reading the verses that describe each of the eight attributes of God as Faithful Companion. As the verses are read, each of you circle one verse under each attribute that is especially meaningful to you. Share your choices with the group.

4. How do you plant yourself in the center of God's will as guided by Romans 12:1-2?

5. When is independence good, and when is it bad?

6. What excuses do you make for not choosing the fruit of the Holy Spirit? (Gal. 5:22-23)

7. Why are qualities like patience more *choices* than something you have or don't have?

8. What heart medicine would God prescribe for you right now according to "How Does Your Heart Respond to Your Companion?"

9. Choose an object in this room and use it to teach the group what doing God's will is. Note it here.

10. Together, decide three actions this group will hold the others accountable for in the area of companionship with God this next week. Write them here.

Group leading tip: Help your group members learn to pray with each other. Never let your goal be to put them on the spot; instead gently teach them. As you vary the format of your prayers from week to week, each member will get to pray in his or her preferred format at least occasionally. Possibilities:

- Let one member write prayer requests while another calls for those requests.
- Invite each member to say one sentence of praise to God for who He is and what He has done.
- Allow members to pray in total silence, you offering a topic, such as "God, we come before you to talk with you about spiritual growth. . ."
- Have each member pray a single sentence or word.
- Partners—divide into pairs for the prayer time.
- In all these, urge your small group to focus on God and listen to Him. They don't have to speak the whole time.

Between You and God

1. What do you like about the opening story in this chapter?

2. How have you experienced each of the eight attributes of God as Companion?

3. Reexamine the eight attributes of God detailed in the section "What Is a Companion?". Then look back over God's attributes in the first three chapters. Make a master list, draw a picture incorporating each, or doodle them—choose whatever recording method helps you remember them.

4. How does companionship with God make you want to do His will? Memorize a verse in this chapter that reminds you of this.

5. How independent are you? Is your type of independence a good thing or a bad thing, and why? What kind of independence honors God rather than resists Him?

6. The fruit of the Spirit is the result of inner workings of the Holy Spirit, but your choice is the other major factor. How will choosing each of these actions help you live that fruit? What other action would help that fruit mature?

Love	Love the Lord and your neighbor (Matt. 22:37-39).
Joy	Rejoice in the Lord (Phil. 4:4).
Peace	Run from evil and do good (1 Pet. 3:11).
Patience	Be patient with everyone (1 Thess. 5:14).
Kindness	Clothe yourself with kindness (Col. 3:12).
Goodness	Do good to all people (Gal. 6:10).
Faithfulness	Be faithful even to the point of death (Rev. 2:10).
Gentleness	Show true humility toward every person (Titus 3:2).
Self-Control	Add to your knowledge, self-control (2 Pet. 1:5).

7. How is your heart toward God? What spiritual report card would God give you, and why?

8. Choose an area of your life in which you want to do God's will. Follow the eight steps under "Why Do You Want to Please Your Companion?"

9. Personal evaluation: On a scale of 1-10 with 10 being total and 1 being not-at-all, rate yourself in each of these commitment areas:

[ ] I obey God out of love rather than fear.
[ ] I have a strong desire to please God in all that I do.
[ ] I am becoming very submissive to the will of God. I do not struggle as much as I used to.
[ ] I read the Bible for understanding.
[ ] I have a clear sense of the presence of God in my life and His love and acceptance of me.
[ ] I have an intensifying desire to draw closer to God, to trust Him more.
[ ] I sense an increase in the intensity and pleasure from my worship and praise of the Lord both publicly and privately.
[ ] There is an increasing amount of self-control, peace, and joy in my life.
[ ] I have a greater feeling of security and confidence in who I am before the Lord.

What things hinder you from saying any of the above statements are true in your relationship with God?

Most of your rankings should be above five to move to the next level.

10. To prepare for the next study, ponder human friends who teach you what God is like, simply through their actions.

drawing closer to God

spiritual intimacy
drawing closer to God

There is a friend who sticks closer than a brother. Prov. 18:24

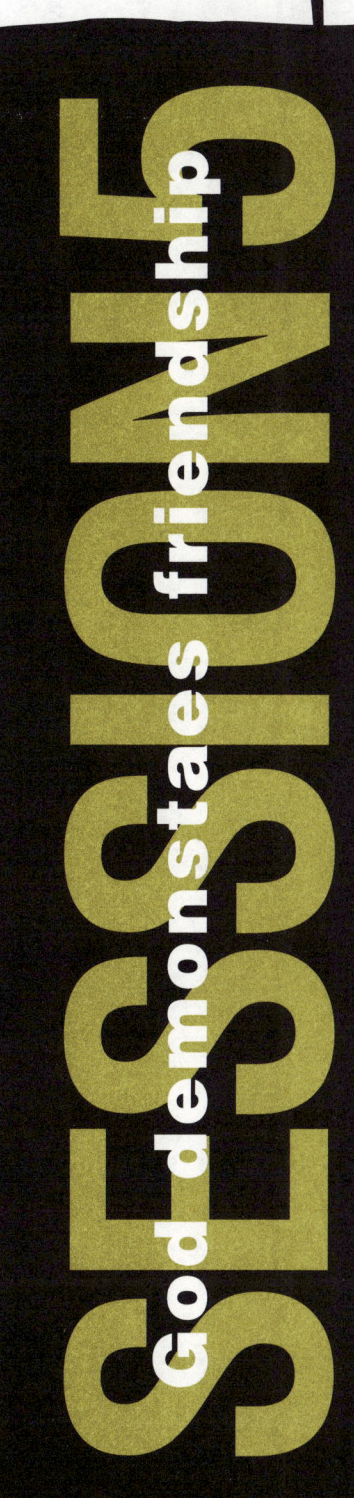

Consider the nature of friendship as it was reflected in the famous television sitcom *Seinfeld.* The bond between the characters Jerry, George, Elaine, and Kramer was a group dynamic rooted in jealousy, rage, insecurity, despair, and a lack of faith in one's fellow human beings. However dysfunctional this bond may be, it offers us a portrait of late-20th-century friendship that is actually more realistic than we would care to admit. Like lots of good friends, Jerry, George, Elaine, and Kramer are aware of each other's strengths and weaknesses. They are united by common interests and desires—for money, for romance, for the perfect apartment. However, you always wonder whether the characters are friends because they choose to be or whether they are just codependent!

Now consider another real life example of friendship, the story of Helen Keller and her teacher, Anne Sullivan. In their true story, as presented in the movie and play *The Miracle Worker,* Anne Sullivan was born half-blind, lost her mother at an early age, and ended up in the poor house. After surgery restored her sight, she devoted herself to the care of the blind. Near this time a nineteen-month-old child, Helen Keller lost both her hearing and her sight. When Helen was a young girl, Anne Sullivan became Helen's teacher. Anne taught Helen to behave and to communicate. She taught Helen language by fingerspelling on her hands. Through Anne's teaching, Helen Keller learned to understand, speak, and communicate. Teacher and pupil remained inseparable for forty-nine years. Helen Keller became famous, along with her teacher.

The time came when Anne's once-healed poor eyesight failed and she became blind again. Anne's favorite student, Helen Keller, now became Anne's teacher. Helen helped her to overcome the lack of sight. Helen taught and cared for her former teacher as devotedly as she herself had been taught. Finally, Helen stood at the deathbed of her good friend Anne. When it was all over, Helen said these words: "I pray for strength to endure the silent dark until she smiles upon me again."

This bond and oneness between Helen Keller and Anne Sullivan, unlike the *Seinfeld* characters, was the result of steady commitment, deep devotion, persistent communication, and mutual friendship. The two loved each other with good-for-the-other care, rather than used each other to validate unhealthy choices.

You can have all these qualities of a good friendship with God. In fact you can go even deeper into friendship because God has no human limitations. God wants to be a Good Friend to you, a friend like you've never known. You can share with God steady commitment, deep devotion, persistent communication, good-for-the-other care, and more. Could this be another piece of the God-puzzle?

Tell about a friendship that validated your unhealthy choices. (Example: You found several friends who would tell you what was wrong was really right.) *The people I worked with at the steakhouse*

Tell about a friend who loved you with good-for-the-other care.
Richard, Will, by, etc...

There is no instant formula for breaking through to the level of Good Friend. But it does build on each of the previous levels: seeing God as Sovereign, Savior, Father and Companion. Grow closer to Him with each day and experience. Your personal and intimate relationship with the God of this universe is exciting and will produce significant benefits that will permeate each area of your life. The benefits of drawing closer to God into a joyful, growing friendship are countless, and a few (You can think of so many more!) are detailed here.

Power in Friendship with God

The first benefit of close friendship with God is God's power. His power has always been there for you, but as God's close friend, you'll understand better how to access it. The Bible is very clear in declaring, *"The people who know their God will display strength and take action"* (Dan. 11:32, NASB). To know God is to understand how and why He works, and to align your efforts with His. As you know God, you become stronger, more powerful, and ready to take action.

To understand this Bible verse, we must understand a little Jewish history. The Jewish people have faced many periods of intense persecution. Probably none of those trials was more devastating than a period under the tyranny of Antichus Epiphanes, the Syrian king who reigned from 175 to 164 B.C. He changed his name to Theos Epiphanes, which means "the manifest God." Because the Jewish people understood his real character, they changed one letter of his name and called him Epimanes, which meant "mad man." He was literally insane with hatred for all Jews.

Daniel was a prophet through whom God told the truth. In the eleventh chapter of his book, God predicted through Daniel the course of events that would take place under the leadership of Antiochus Epiphanes. He was 100 percent accurate. Antiochus Epiphanes ordered Jewish sacrifices to stop. He desecrated the temple by offering a pig on the altar. He prohibited the observance of the Sabbath and the circumcision of children. He set up idolatrous altars and ordered all copies of the Scriptures destroyed. Anyone who disobeyed Antiochus Ephipanes incurred his wrath in the form of an ancient holocaust. How would the Jewish people survive?

Daniel knew: *The people who know their God would display strength and take action.*

This is exactly what happened. The Maccabees led a heroic revolt against Antiochus. They knew their God and they claimed His power. Christians today have at their disposal the same degree of courage and power. They grow it through knowing God, and deliberately drawing on His power. There is no other way to gain this spiritual power except through an intimate knowledge of God—an experiential as well as intellectual understanding.

How does God want you to live as a person of power?

Why is God's power stronger than violence, popularity, wealth, politics, or any other commonly recognized power?

Peace in Friendship with God

The second spiritual benefit of friendship with God is personal peace, a sense of well-being that no external circumstance can shake. Peter explained this very important occurrence in people with a deepening relationship with God. He said, *"Grace and peace be yours in abundance through the knowledge of God and of Jesus our Lord"* (2 Pet. 1:2). Both grace and peace become yours in increasing amounts as you act on your increasing knowledge of God. For example, when you know that calm answers turn away anger, you talk disagreements out calmly. The resulting solution gives you and the other person peace, without any regret over what you said or didn't say.

Peace is inner tranquillity, a quiet confidence, an ability to stay under control in spite of the circumstances that confront you. In a world seemingly coming apart at the seams, Christians who are drawing closer to God have a unique peace available to them. Therefore, as CrossSeekers, we can turn worry into actions that solve the problem. We can deliberately enjoy the comfort of life with God.

How do you experience inner peace?

Wisdom Drawn from Friendship with God

The third spiritual benefit of friendship with God is wisdom. You will discover how to apply truth to everyday circumstances. Paul, of the New Testament, often prayed that his followers would learn more about the advantages of a deeper walk with the Lord. For Christians in Ephesus he prayed, *"I keep asking that the God of our Lord Jesus Christ, the glorious Father, may give you the Spirit of wisdom and rev-*

elation, so that you may know him better" (Eph. 1:17). In this verse the word "Spirit" is not a direct reference to the Holy Spirit. It refers to a mental disposition of genuine spiritual understanding that can only come from the Holy Spirit. These Christians already had the indwelling Holy Spirit. Now Paul wanted them to grasp the spiritual realities available to them and appropriate these truths in their lives.

Some people feel inadequate in spiritual understanding. They read the Word of God, but have difficulty understanding it. They may totally miss the appropriate application in their lives. Where is this spirit of wisdom to be found? In the knowledge of Christ. This knowledge is not just head knowledge, but shared experience. The people who experience God as Good Friend will have a deepening spiritual understanding despite any lack of theological training. The time they spend with Him provides insight and purpose of life.

Growth Resulting from Friendship with God

The fourth spiritual benefit of friendship with God is growth. *"For this reason, since the day we heard about you, we have not stopped praying for you and asking God to fill you will the knowledge of his will through all spiritual wisdom and understanding. And we pray this in order that you may live a life worthy of the Lord and may please him in every way: bearing fruit in every good work, growing in the knowledge of God"* (Col. 1:9-10). Do you understand what Paul has said? The knowledge of God is the means by which we bear fruit and increase in every good work God wants us to accomplish. The knowledge of God gives us not only understanding of how to do good, but power to carry out that understanding.

As CrossSeekers we need more than knowledge about the truths of the Bible. We need understanding of why God does what He does. This helps us understand His character, and enjoy His presence. It shows us how to obey God even when the circumstances don't appear black and white. When we understand God's reasons and character, we can walk in accordance with Him. The more we know of His love for us, the more we will love Him in return. As John wrote in 1 John 4:19: *"We love because he first loved us."*

Psychologists tell us that we develop similarities to the people with whom we spend the most time. Likewise, as we spend more time with our Savior, grow in our knowledge of Him, and develop Christlikeness, we become more like Him. We will bear fruit and good works because of our knowledge and intimacy with God. The closer we are to Him, the more we will enjoy life and the more we will grow in our relationship with Jesus. This is the ultimate goal of our life: to be like Jesus.

Four Actions That Bring Friendship with God

So how do you grow from companionship to even deeper friendship with God? *First, live a lifestyle of confession.* This is not simply reciting all your inadequacies and insufficiencies. It is not displaying your dirty laundry for everyone else to examine and critique. It is the opportunity to examine who is really in charge and continually assess your perspective.

David wrote in Psalm 139:1-4, 23-24:
> *"O Lord, you have searched me and you know me. You know when I sit and when I rise; you perceive my thoughts from afar. You discern my going out and my lying down; you are familiar with all my ways. Before a word is on my tongue you know it completely, O Lord…Search me, O God, and know my heart; test me and know my anxious thoughts. See if there is any offensive way in me, and lead me in the way everlasting."*

What changes are necessary in your life? What actions do you need to keep? What patterns can you deepen? What new ones can you develop? Where have you been selfish or piggish? What do you need to confess to God? About what do you need to rejoice with Him?

Second, to grow from companionship to even deeper friendship with God, live a lifestyle of obedience. At this Good Friend level, your obedience will be based on a deep love for God and a desire to do His will. The closeness you experience with God is walking arm-in-arm. It would be impossible for two, linked arm-in-arm, to walk with much distance between them or to go in different directions. There is definite agreement, and since the Lord cannot walk a wrong road, CrossSeekers will find the right road by walking with Him. Whatever He asks, you joyfully do. On rare occasions you may have a reservation about what He says. You may hesitate as you mull over the desirability of doing this difficult thing He asks of you. But you go ahead and do it.

The third way to grow from companionship to even deeper friendship with God is to develop a heart of joy. This happens as you let your heart respond to God. Joy also comes from opportunity to serve God. Before, you may have served God as an imposition. Now, you consider service a privilege.

A fourth way to grow from companionship to deeper friendship with God is stark-raving honesty. Until we are totally honest with ourselves and God, we will put up blocks against moving any deeper in our relationship with God as Good Friend. Pride, fear, and guilt will continue to hinder our relationship with God.

What's the difference between *confession,* and a *life of confession*?

What brings you joy?

> *Questions to Evaluate Whether Something Fits God's Standards*
>
> *Wondering if a relationship, an action, an attitude, or a commitment fits God's standards for you? Ask these questions, and invite a trusted spiritually mature adult to tell you how he or she would answer these questions for you in this area:*
> - *Is it edifying?*
> - *Does it compromise to the world's standards?*
> - *Is it a form of rationalization, or actually what needs to happen?*
> - *How are my emotions responding?*

Encourage Your Group: Actions for Group Study

1. How is the friendship between Helen Keller and Anne Sullivan happier and healthier than the friendship group on *Seinfield*?

2. Discuss the three questions at the end of the introductory section. Jot what you learn from the discussion here.

3. How have you seen Daniel 11:32 exhibited on your campus?

4. How is wisdom different than knowledge? Can a college student be wise, or do you have to have lived most of your life to be truly wise? (See Eph. 1:17.)

5. Name something God does that confuses you. Invite the group to explain why He does this, so you can understand better. (Be biblical in your explanations rather than guessing.)

6. Which of the "Four Actions That Bring Friendship with God" do you most need right now, and why?

7. How do we relate to God differently than we relate to a human friend?

8. Has your relationship with God become less shallow and superficial through this study? How?

9. In what ways are you still keeping up pretenses with God and others concerning your spiritual life?

10. How can we CrossSeekers hold each other accountable for solid friendships with both people and God? How can we do this without being judgmental?

Group leading tip: Show your group how to genuinely listen to one another. Ask: Listening is too often impatient-waiting-until-I-can-share-my-views-and-ideas. How can we give each other genuine attention with the goal of understanding what the other person has to say?

To help your listening skills in your small group:
- Be courteous. You will have your chance to talk later.
- Keep eye contact.
- Listen intently. Pay attention and stay alert.
- Listen to what is not said. Watch the person's body language and facial expressions.
- Ask open-ended questions and draw people into the discussion.

The members of your small group will participate more when they know you are listening to them.

Between You and God

1. Think of several friendships you've had, both healthy and unhealthy ones. How is friendship with God like and unlike these relationships?

2. How have you seen each of the four benefits of friendship with God grow in your life? The four are power, peace, wisdom, and growth.

3. What power have you accessed as you have drawn close to God? (Examples: power to be patient, power to insist someone do the right thing, power to right a wrong, power to wait, more)

4. How would you explain how to develop peace? Pretend you are speaking to a new Christian.

5. Read and then memorize Ephesians 1:17.

6. Why is it true that we develop similarities to the people with whom we spend the most time?

7. How has God personally made each of these easy for you: Confession? Obedience? Joy? Honesty?

8. Why is God definitely a friend but definitely more than a friend?

9. Name one specific way you have grown and progressed in your relationship with God through this study.

10. Personal evaluation: This one is the longest evaluation yet. On a scale of 1-10 with 10 being total and 1 being not-at-all, rate yourself on where you are in each of these commitment areas:

[ ] I have a deep love for God and desire to do His will 100 percent of the time.
[ ] I see God stripping away from my life many unnecessary things. This pleases me.
[ ] I serve God from a willing heart.
[ ] The Scriptures are alive and meaningful to me.
[ ] Praise and worship are very important to me.
[ ] I attend church not just for the fellowship, but because of my great love for the Lord.
[ ] My faith is such that it would be almost impossible for anyone to be able to undermine it or keep me from following God's will in any given situation.
[ ] I have regular, scheduled times with the Lord. They are very important to me.
[ ] I seek to know and follow the will of God even in what others would consider trivial matters.

[ ] With all my heart, I desire to walk free from sin.
[ ] It grieves me when I sin.
[ ] There is rarely or never an instance when I plan to sin (such as thinking about how to deceive or lie to someone, steal, or to "get away" with some act).
[ ] Hearing gossip grieves me.
[ ] I avoid gossiping at all costs.
[ ] I have a real peace in my life no matter what is going on around me. I stay focused on God.
[ ] I want God to help me remove every weakness I have.
[ ] I use praise and worship even when I'm not with a group.
[ ] I have a real sense of God's presence in my life at all times. I talk to Him much of the day.
[ ] My conversation with God is not always talking about my needs. Often it includes expressions of gratefulness for creation and those He has brought into my life.

Your honest self-eveluation should include a score of above 5 on at least seventeen items to advance to the next level.

11. To prepare for the next study, think about how your values compare to God's: How does what blesses you bless God? How does what upsets you upset God?

drawing closer to God

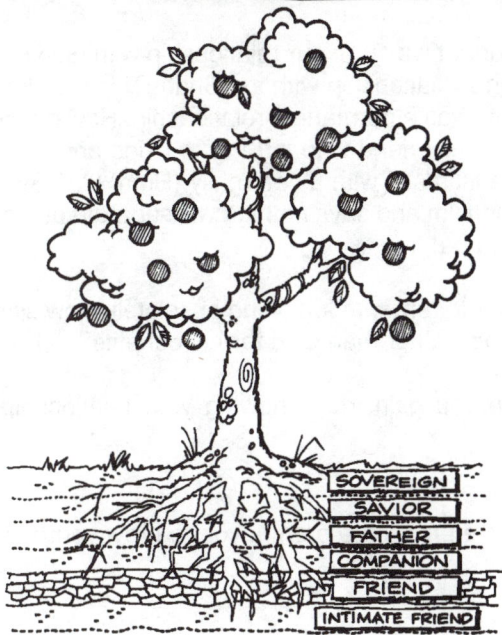

I have called you friends, for everything that I learned from my Father I have made known to you. John 15:15

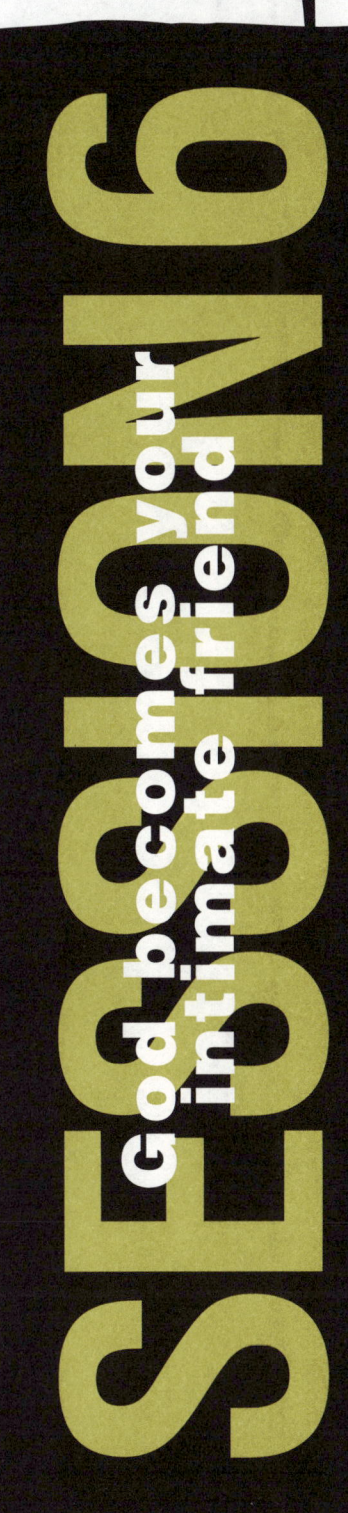

SESSION 6
God becomes your intimate friend

The story is told of Shah Abbis, a Persian monarch who loved his people very much. To know and understand them better, he would mingle with his subjects in various disguises. One day, disguised as a poor man, he went to the public baths. In a tiny cellar, he sat beside the fireman who tended the furnace. When it was mealtime, the monarch shared this man's coarse food and talked to this lonely subject as a friend.

Again and again Shah Abbis visited the fireman. The firemen grew to love the monarch without figuring out who he was. One day the Shah told him he was the monarch, expecting the man to ask for some gift from him. But the fireman sat gazing at the ruler with love and wonder and at last spoke; "You left your palace and your glory to sit with me in this dark place, to eat of my coarse food, to care whether my heart was glad or sorry. On others you may bestow rich presents, but to me you have given yourself, and it only remains for me to pray that you will never withdraw the gift of your friendship."

As CrossSeekers, this is how our relationship with the Lord should be. We can want God for who He is, not what He can do for us, or give us, or make us into.

There's an important way that our relationship with God can be different from the fireman's relationship with the Shah: This man knew there was no guarantee this was a permanent relationship. How different it is for us as we walk with our Friend who is King of kings and Lord of lords. He wants to walk in intimacy with us eternally (Rom. 8:38-39). He chose to draw us closer to Him and says nothing will separate us from Him. What a secure place to be!

On a scale of one to ten, with ten being absolutely, how sincerely do you want God for God, rather than God for his benefits?

What delight do you gain from knowing your relationship with God is eternal?

How does God's eternal care prompt you to grow your relationship with Him?

Intimacy in Knowing God

You have recognized God as Sovereign, Savior, Father, Companion, and Friend. Now you can go to the deepest level of all: Intimate Friend. Intimacy is total closeness, a full trust and complete sharing of life. Enoch walked and talked with God. Abraham was a friend of God. David was a man after God's own heart. Moses talked with God face to face. And now you can choose to be an intimate friend of God. The God-puzzle may be almost complete with this piece of the puzzle.

Our culture explains intimacy in many ways. We use it in phrases like "an intimate dinner for two," meaning a close, memorable dinner. When we talk about an intimate friendship, we indicate a close, deep relationship. When we use it with God, we describe a closeness that is wed with understanding, confidence, and total acceptance. An intimate friendship with God treasures these attributes of God: tenderhearted, gentle, great heart of love, complete ability to meet every need and care, totally good, wants the very best for me, and is committed to me.

Intimacy with God is no longer theory but experience. It is faith based in reality. You are in awe of who God is, what He is, and who you are to Him. You are overwhelmed and humbled with the amount of love you feel from God. Words are weak and incapable of catching the thrill, joy, and pleasure of having such a close relationship with the Lord.

The intimate friend level may be compared to seeing colors. The person who is colorblind may see only black and white with tones of gray. Viewing a sunset can be a totally different experience for those who see color and those who do not. They all see the same sky, but one group experiences a richer, deeper, more exciting quality to the view. They are able to see many brilliant colors and their infinite hues. Those in the other group understand there is something there. But unless they see color, they never truly or fully appreciate a sunset.

What color highlights intimacy with God?
What texture feels like intimacy with God?
What words picture intimacy with God?

Listen to the song "Deeper" on the album *King of Fools* by delirious? (Curious? Music U.K., 1997).

- Fill in the blank:
"I want to be _____ be a help to the strong."

What does this mean?

Riches in Matching Your Values with God's

Intimacy brings you and your loved one into such close proximity that it is as if you are one—intellectually, emotionally, experientially, and more. Perhaps most clearly your intimacy with God will show in your values. How do your values compare to God's? What blesses you? What upsets you? What takes up your time? What do you worry about? If you lie awake sleepless, what is it that keeps you awake? In other words, what are your values?

You may list things like friends, family, meaningful work, and interesting discoveries. These values become your priorities. Your priorities determine what you do with your time and resources, and more importantly, when you will do it. For example, because you value meaningful work, you study hard during the afternoon hours. Then your grades will be high enough to graduate and qualify for meaningful work. Your daytime study frees you to be with friends and go to Bible study during evening hours.

Priorities determine whether or not you will get the job done. It is easy to get so busy talking to friends, or messing with email, or even going to Bible studies, that you fail to grapple with the big projects, pressing issues, and heartaches. Let your values help you deliberately budget your time, talents, and treasures. Schedule things that take the most time and concentration first, followed by smaller projects, followed by easy-to-enjoy things. One person described it as a huge jar being your life. Put the boulders in first, then the pea gravel, and then the sand. The pea gravel settles into the empty spaces around the boulders. Then the sand fills the spots left by the pea gravel. If you start with sand, the big things will never fit. And if you only do the big things, you miss filling your life with God's simple pleasures. God calls deliberate time use stewardship—it's a great way to demonstrate your faith.

Those with an intimate friendship with God want to contribute to God's kingdom. They choose to focus on what counts for eternity, to minister for God in everything they do. Consider friendships. Some friends, even Christian ones, are fun but have little desire to gain life skills or focus on hard-to-do things. They miss some of God's deepest joys—the joys of sticking with a challenge until you master it. Spending less time with these friends, and more with those who show stick-to-itiveness is a way to invest in eternity. Such friends will help you master school and enjoy life more persistently.

Once you place your priorities under God, some things will have to go. Anything with even a hint of being outside the will of the Lord will get in the way. Reject it. As a CrossSeeker, ask about everything you do or say, "Is it squeaky clean?" Purposely choose to set aside your right to rationalize or give excuses for doing anything. If it is questionable, it is out of bounds. Do this with a heart of love for the Lord. Choose to do nothing to grieve or disappoint Him.

When you place your priorities under God, you will experience good, unexpected pleasures. You'll find deeper friendships when you choose friends who also walk with God as Intimate Friend. You'll find greater joy at the little things—good conversations, interesting learning, delightful laughter. You'll find joy in choosing the squeaky clean activities, stuff that brings fun long after the activity itself is over. You'll find that tiny obediences, like saying a kind word to someone you don't usually talk to, pay off in huge benefits.

As a college student, you have twenty-four hours of time and resources that include your interests and talents. How does God want you to use these to communicate what really matters in life?

Freedom to Choose Servanthood

As an intimate friend of God, you serve God with joy. You serve with physical actions like encouragement, witnessing, and helping. You serve with unseen actions like prayer for matters far beyond your own family interest or sphere of influence. Such works are a natural outflow of your intimate walk with God.

As a friend of God, you care about what is on the heart of God. You hurt when God hurts. You take offense at what offends God. You rejoice when God rejoices.

What do you value that God values? List some common values here.

> **Reset Your Priorities**
>
> *If you want to find out what is really important, ask yourself what someone else should complete if you died suddenly. The priorities of the Christian life have a definite bearing on how much intimacy we are going to have with God.*

Nourishment to Walk Together through Dry Times

Intimacy with God does not mean continual happiness. It means continual company. Mountaintop experiences have valleys on both sides. Show your godly character and steady faith in both the big crises of life and the small crises of life. Christians are a lot like tea bags. Nobody really knows what's on the inside, until we are in hot water.

Maybe someone forgot the good things you did for him or her. As a CrossSeeker, find comfort in the fact that God notices. Or maybe you forgot what God has done for you. Make a personalized list of different things that have been meaningful to you in your relationship with God. Include verses of Scripture, songs, poems, prayers, thoughts, and more. Read this list the next time you face a dry spell to remind yourself of God's goodness and faithfulness. Then take actions like those suggested in "Solutions to Dryness."

How much do you trust God—really trust Him? If you mean real business with God, you trust that He wants only the best for you and you can depend upon Him even during dry times. One way to express this is to draw up a blank contract.

Write:

"Dear Father, I love You and trust You with every area of my life. Do with my life as You wish. Fill in the rest of this page with whatever You want for my life, and I will do it."

Finally, sign your name at the bottom with the date.

You may find yourself in a battle of the mind as you write a contract like this. You may think:

> This is crazy. Who knows what God may ask of me! Am I opening up the door for Him to make me marry a "dog," give me cancer or AIDS?

> Of course not! I know God is the God of Light (1 John 1:5) and doesn't do things like that. Even so, total surrender seems way too risky. What if he sends me to Africa? Well, then it must be a good plan.

> My head knows this, but my heart's not sure! What if I let God show me what He wants first, then I can decide whether or not to do it? That is the safest way. But is it? If God actually knows the future, isn't He the best one to decide whether or not to do it? Shouldn't I be showing Him what I want and letting Him decide?

> If I sign this and He asks me to do something weird, I'm stuck. But God's not weird. So I don't have to worry about Him making me do something weird. Contracting with Him is brilliant, and safe, and good.

Such thoughts go with the drawing closer process. You sort out what is temptation and what is from God. You wrestle with your fears to sort truth from fantasy. You discover through this internal dialogue that God is good, and trusting Him is good.

When your heart's desire is to do a certain thing and negative thoughts flood your mind, invite God to help you sort them through. Discover why you can trust God no matter what. When any reservations come, deal with them. God will help you.

Use the space on the following page to jot down a dialogue between you and God, talking over an area in which you struggle.

Solutions to Dryness

1. When your eyes are on circumstances, talk to God about those circumstances. He'll help you know what to do.
2. When you're self-centered, choose to become God-centered.
3. When you feel unfulfilled, sharpen your decision-making skills. Notice what bugs you and discover what God wants you to do about it.
4. When prayer becomes routine, pray in a different place, and at one more time.
5. When you're hiding a sin, confess it to God and stop it with God's power.
6. When someone has come between you and the Lord, change that relationship to give God back His rightful place.
7. When something else, even a ministry project, comes between you and God, move past that something to snuggle up to God.
8. When pride in your relationship with the Lord gets you off track, choose to worship God rather than gloat in him.
9. When you judge others, ask God to help you be patient with them.
10. When you judge your relationship with God by your feelings and not by what is truth, tell Satan to quit undermining your confidence in God.

Confidence That God Will Get You Through

God has the power to help you overcome any and every circumstance. Romans 8:28 says, *"In all things God works for the good of those who love him, who have been called according to his purpose."* This does not say everything is good, but that God works in and around everything to do good. Nothing, even the ugliest of events, can stop God from doing good. So peek past ugliness to see the good God continues to do. When someone gets cancer, that is not good. When someone is abused, that is not good. So refuse to bless the bad and insult God by saying, "This must be something that God is going to use for good." God doesn't use bad. That goes against his nature. Instead he works around bad to continue bringing good.

In Moses' life, God provided a way to bring sweetness after a bitter experience. God had parted the Red Sea for the Israelites three day earlier. Now they wallowed in self-pity because the water in the area (Marah) was bitter. Exodus 15:25 states, *"Then Moses cried out to the Lord, and the Lord showed him a piece of wood. He threw it into the water, and the water became sweet. There the Lord made a decree and a law for them, and there he tested them."*

God showed Moses the wood. Why? Because he knew the solution. When we look at ourselves and focus on only on our problems, we can't see God's answers. Often God meets our needs in ways that go far beyond our expectations. Read Exodus 15:27: *"Then they came to Elim, where there were twelve springs and seventy palm trees, and they camped there near the water."* Right in the middle of miles and miles of barren desert, God provided an oasis.

How far is Elim from Marah? Five to ten miles. The Israelites had stopped too soon. So remember not to quit and give up on your intimate relationship with God. The solution to your problem may be just five miles away. Keep moving despite your feelings. There will be days when you say, "I'm tired. I don't feel like serving anymore. I don't feel like praying anymore. I don't like going to church. I don't like reading my Bible." What do you do when you don't feel like doing those things? You do them.

Most of the great things in life are done by people who did not feel like doing them. Then through doing these good things, good happens. So daily do God's good!

In what areas of your walk with the Lord do you need to be held accountable for by the group?

How will you as a group continue to be committed to one another?

Encourage Your Group: Actions for Group Study

1. How are you like and unlike the fireman in the opening story?

2. What are the six levels of closeness with God? Why is each important to you?

3. How do your values compare to God's?

4. How can even small actions have eternal significance (contribute to God's kingdom both now and in the future)?

5. What questions do you ask yourself to decide whether an action is good or bad to do?

6. Why are some things bad to do just because of the time you pick to do them? (Sample: Talking on the phone when you should be studying keeps you from honoring God with good learning.)

7. How does knowing God's heart help you serve Him?

8. How have you grown close to God in good times?

9. How have you grown closer to God in bad times?

When have you had a battle of the mind like that under "Nourishment to Walk Together through Dry Times?" How did it help you grow more able to trust Him?

10. Romans 8:28 and 8:38-39 go hand in hand. Why?

11. Answer together the questions at the end of this chapter.

Group leading tip: Spirituality is the power to change the atmosphere to God-focus by one's presence. Help your group members be spiritual by encouraging them to choose every action and word to glorify God.

Between You and God

1. What do you like about the story about Shah Abbis and the fireman?

2. How is intimacy with God like seeing colors?

3. How is intimacy with God like and unlike intimacy with a human?

4. What blesses you?

What upsets you?

What takes up your time?

When you lie awake sleepless, what is it that keeps you awake?

How do each of these match, or need to be modified to more closely to match God's values?

5. How can you tell the difference between something with eternal significance and something of temporary significance?

6. The more our hearts are touched with what God cares about, the better we know what to give our time to. Why?

7. What action will you take to overcome each of these obstacles to intimacy with God: Laziness? Impatience? Rationalization and excuses? Wrong motives?

8. Write a contract of devotion to God. Use it in your prayer time today, and put it in a place you'll see it daily.

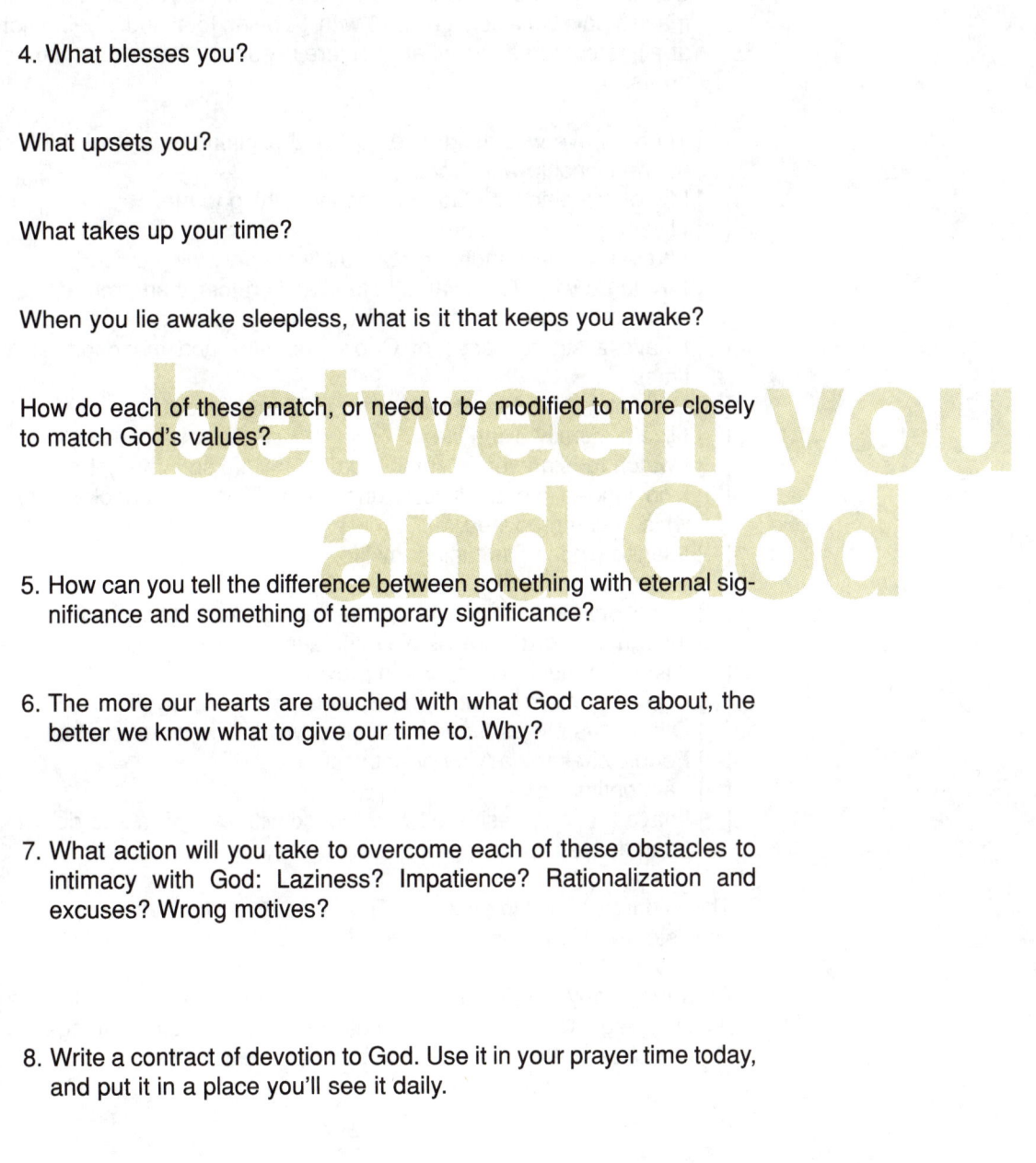

9. Read John 15. Choose at least one verse to memorize.

10. Complete this personal evaluation as a crown to your Spiritual Intimacy study. On a scale of 1-10 with 10 being total and 1 being not-at-all, rate yourself on where you are in each of these commitment areas:

[ ] There is overwhelming awe, joy, and excitement when I think of my relationship with God.
[ ] My relationship with God means everything to me.
[ ] I live to please the Lord.
[ ] I have joy in surrendering absolutely to every wish of God.
[ ] I try to do what God wants immediately rather than procrastinate or try to find a way around what I know He wants.
[ ] I have a strong sense of God's presence and friendship at all times.
[ ] I do not withhold anything in my life from the Lord.
[ ] I live a morally clean life.
[ ] I watch for sin even in small areas of my life so I can get rid of it.
[ ] I no longer tolerate little wrong things I once overlooked or in which I compromised.
[ ] I sense God is fine tuning my life.

[ ] I find prayer is a constant flow throughout the day, almost as though the Lord were visible beside me.
[ ] I listen as much as I speak in prayer.
[ ] I sense that each fruit of the Spirit is present in my life.
[ ] Others see me as a person of great wisdom and self-control.
[ ] People seek my advice or counsel.
[ ] I am optimistic.
[ ] I have a strong desire to live at peace with everyone and do what I can to live this way.

This is our last level to evaluate. This is the level we want to attain and consistently stay in.

On a trip, many people take notes so they can remember their experiences. Begin to record your spiritual journey. Write all the things that God teaches you as you continue to draw closer to Him.

Listen

Listen to the song "Real" on the album *Considering Lily* by Considering Lily (ForeFront, 1997).

- **What circumstances make it difficult to be "real"?**

- **List some ways CrossSeekers can be "real."**

In general, we are the best-equipped bunch of Christians who ever came down the path of history. We have more gadgets, equipment, and money per capita than most of the people who have gone before us. Yet society in general still reaches for more. What are the real values? What is even more valuable than things?

When you as a CrossSeeker choose to let wrong things go and right things come, you will find that others follow you. Your deliberate actions for Jesus encourage others to do the same. How have you seen this happen?

Who have you followed because of their genuine letting wrong things go and right things come?

Drawing close to God is real. It is happening in your life as a CrossSeeker because of who God is, and your genuine desire to be close to Him.

The puzzle pieces are interlocked, and you see the picture. Hopefully, because of this study, you now see God more clearly. Draw closer to Him!

Continue to learn more about God and grow in your relationship with Him as a CrossSeeker. Information about other resources for you and your CrossSeekers Covenant group are located in the back of this book.

leader's guide

spiritual intimacy

drawing closer to God

Spiritual Intimacy: Drawing Closer to God is a six-week collegiate and young adult study based on *Drawing Closer* by Glen Martin & Dian Ginter. Together you and your group-mates can discover just how to walk through life with our wonderfully personal God.

Introduction to this Study
This study explores the following questions:
- How does God reveal Himself to me?
- What is God like?
- Why did God come to earth?
- How does the Savior's love impact my love?
- What does God teach me about true fatherhood?
- What distortions cloud my picture of God? How will I erase and redraw?
- Why do I want God's companionship?
- Why does obedience bring true freedom?
- How is God like and unlike a human friend?
- How is friendship with God related to personal peace? To spiritual understanding?
- How does intimacy with God show in everyday life?
- How do my values compare to God's—what blesses me? Upsets me? Takes up my time? Keeps me awake at night?

Leader Qualifications
- **Be curious**—Desire to know God and to discover how to live for Him.
- **Be interested**—Show the people in your group that you care about the details of their daily lives.
- **Be constant**—Lead each of the six sessions by showing a caring spirit, by starting and ending on time.
- **Be in contact**—with God, with His Word, with the people in your group.
- **Be watchful**—Notice when God is teaching you and your group members. Don't miss His lessons.
- **Be responsive**—Answer God's call to make new insights a part of your daily walk.
- **Be positive**—Use humor, joy, enthusiasm, and your spiritual gifts. Make it easy for each group member to do the same.
- **Be un-preachy**—This is a reminder not to lecture and preach. Instead guide your students to share life and learn with each other.

Guidelines for Effective Group Study Time

1. Choose six weeks that allow the greatest participation. Sometimes this means starting the week students arrive on campus, before they've had time to get involved in so many activities. Other times it means getting the group together later, opening calendars and together choosing a day, time, and place to meet each week.

2. Start on time. This encourages the whole group to be on time.

3. End on time. This lets busy students know they can get right back to finishing that school paper, or studying for that test.

4. Allow an hour to 90 minutes for each weekly session.

5. Challenge your group to read and complete that week's study before coming together to discuss it.

6. During the session, keep the discussion centered on the study. Jot stray subjects on paper—See the #8 "Issue Bin" under "During the Session" below.

7. Covenant together that all things shared in the group are to be kept in ABSOLUTE CONFIDENTIALITY . . . TOP SECRET. . .CLASSIFIED. What's said in the group stays in the group. Only with this trust and respect can openness and transparency happen.

8. Encourage all to share. Everyone-shares-one-sentence and similar safe-sharing strategies allow all to participate without making any feel overly vulnerable.

9. Encourage all members to bring their own Bibles so they can mark them as they make discoveries during the session.

During the Session

1. Your job is to facilitate the discussion. With key questions and purposeful waiting, get everyone involved and keep the discussion flowing. Questions throughout the studies and under "Encourage Your Group" in each study will help with this process.

2. Open each session with prayer. Vary the ways you do this. Sometimes you or a group member will pray a line or two. Other times you'll ask a group member to write requests while others share them. Then close this open-eyed prayer with an "amen."

3. Introduce a no-slam rule. Insist that group members never put down another's comment, idea, or concern. Instead, prompt the active encouragement detailed in Hebrews 10:24-25.

4. Be sensitive to the fact that participating in a group can be scary. Members wonder, "Will what I say be told to others?" "What will others think of my failures and struggles?" "Will they think less of me, or ridicule me?" A small group must be a secure place where participants trust each other and encourage each other. The no-slam rule (#3) and ground rules like these provide a good basis for this:

a. Respect the privacy of each person. Do not repeat outside the group what anyone says in the group
    b. Insist that everyone participate so no one has to worry about volunteering (see suggestion #6 below). If participation is expected, it becomes safer to participate.
    c. Equalize talking. Encourage each group member to talk about as much as he or she listens. Urge them to refuse to dominate or stay too quiet.
    d. Do not try to "fix" others with advice or suggestions. Instead stick to your own experiences and insights, with a great respect and an absence of criticism for the member who shares.
    e. Do not interrupt someone else as he/she shares.

5. Use open-ended questions to encourage talking and thinking. An open-ended question requires more than a yes-or-no answer, and different than a pat answer. These open ended questions work with almost every passage:

- What do you think was the main message of this session?
- What insights did you gain as you worked through this material before coming today?
- What experiences did the author share that you can relate to?
- What Bible passage relates to you most strongly right now? Why?
- How will you live this passage?
- How does this session prompt you to draw closer to God?
- What issues surfaced as you studied that you know you need to address? How do you plan to address them?

6. Make it easy to share with strategies like everyone-around-the-circle-give-an-idea and speak-an-insight-in-alphabetical-order-of-first-name. When everyone shares in sequence, sharing becomes more comfortable and unanimous.

7. Lead the group in the "Encourage Your Group" activities at the end of each chapter, as well as the activities within the main text.

8. If your group gets sidetracked on issues, jot these down and place them in the "Issue Bin," a box or paper bag you bring along. Then you can:

    a. Have an additional meeting just to discuss the issues listed.
    b. Meet for an optional few minutes early the next week to tackle an issue placed in the box or bag.
    c. Suggest students talk those over after the study as schedules permit.

9. Close by prompting group members to complete the "Between You and God" section privately.

10. Close in prayer.

Crossseekers Resources

CrossSeekers: Discipleship Covenant for a New Generation
by Henry Blackaby and Richard Blackaby

Discover the six CrossSeekers principles brought to life in a user-friendly, practical, story-telling format. This study sets the stage for an exploration of each CrossSeekers Covenant point. Biblical and contemporary examples of promises made, promises kept, and promises broken, along with consequences, bring the biblical truths home to today's college students.
• 9 sessions • Interactive in format • Leader's helps included • $8.95
• ISBN 0-7673-9084-9

CrossSeekers: Transparent Living, Living a Life of Integrity
by Rod Handley

Integrity. Everyone talks about it. God *delights* in it. We *demand* it. But what exactly *is* integrity, and is it important? If you want to be a person of integrity, to live the kind of life Christ modeled—to speak the truth in love, to stand firm in your convictions, to be honest and trustworthy, then *Transparent Living, Living a Life of Integrity* is for you! This study supports the CrossSeekers Covenant principle *integrity.* • 6 sessions • Leader's guide included • $6.95
• ISBN 0-7673-9296-5

CrossSeekers: Soul Food for Relationships, Developing Christlike Relationships
by J. Keith Miller

Our relationships with other people are key to happiness and success in life. Too often, though, these relationships become stressful and unhealthy. How can we keep them Christlike? J. Keith Miller examines the false personality we create that leaves us feeling lonely, fearful, doubtful. Confronting this constructed personality and dismantling the self-created aspects lead us to authentic living and Christlike relationships. This study supports the CrossSeekers Covenant principle *Christlike relationships.*
• 6 sessions • Leader's guide included • $6.95 • ISBN 0-7673-9426-7

CrossSeekers: Holy and Acceptable, Building a Pure Temple
by Dave Edwards

First Corinthians 6 tells us that our bodies are temples of the Holy Spirit. But what does that mean, and why should we care? This study looks at what it means for us to be God's temple. Through Bible study and contemporary situations, the physical, mental, and spiritual aspects are explored, along with their interrelatedness, as well as what to do when you fail in your pursuit of purity. This study supports the CrossSeekers Covenant principle *purity.*
• 6 sessions • Interactive in format • Leader's guide included • $6.95
• ISBN 0-7673-9428-3

CrossSeekers: Fearless, Sharing an Authentic Witness
by William Fay and Dean Finley

Fearless, Sharing an Authentic Witness will equip collegians for sharing their faith with others. Sessions address concepts such as our lives as a living witness (using the CrossSeekers Covenant points for discussion), how Jesus shared with persons He met, learning where God is at work in another person's life, a threat-free and effective method for presenting the gospel, and addressing difficult questions/situations. Based on *Share Jesus Without Fear*, this study supports the CrossSeekers Covenant principle *witness*.
• 6 sessions • Interactive in format • Leader's guide included • $6.95
• Available 7/99 • ISBN 0-7673-9865-3

CrossSeekers: Gifted! Serving in Christ's Name

Gifted! Serving in Christ's Name examines spiritual gifts given by the Holy Spirit to each believer and leads collegians to discover their gifts and how to use them in service for Christ. A spiritual gifts inventory is included to enable collegians to determine their gifts. Collegians using their gifts in various service will be profiled, and opportunities for service will be highlighted. Collegians will be challenged to find a place of service utilizing their gifts. This study supports the CrossSeekers Covenant principle *service*.
• 6 sessions • Interactive in format • Leader's guide included • $6.95
• Available 7/99 • ISBN 0-7673-9853-X

Followology @ Collegiate Ministry: Following Jesus in the Real World
by Allen Jackson

How well do you follow as a Christian? *Followology* is designed for the college student or young adult who is serious about following Jesus. Through an informal, interactive study, collegians will learn to follow the One who knows the way, because He *is* the Way! • 8 sessions • Interactive in format • Leader's helps included • $9.95 • ISBN 0-7673-9083-0

Transitions: Preparing for College
compiled by Art Herron

For high school juniors and seniors *and their parents*. Practical help for the transition from high school to college—the admissions process, financial aid, loans and scholarships, lifestyle changes, spiritual development, and more!
• 6 sessions • Leader's helps included • $7.95 • ISBN 0-7673-9082-2

For more information, visit our Web site: www.crossseekers.org.